*Building a Caring-Sharing Community
of Believers*

Building a Caring-Sharing Community of Believers

by

Elvin M. Powers

Beacon Hill Press of Kansas City
Kansas City, Missouri

Copyright 1983
by Beacon Hill Press of Kansas City

ISBN: 0-8341-0822-4

Printed in the United States of America

Cover by: Royce Ratcliff

Permissions to quote from the following copyrighted versions of the Bible are acknowledged with appreciation:
The Holy Bible, New International Version (NIV), copyright © 1978 by New York International Bible Society.
The Living Bible (TLB), © 1971 by Tyndale House Publishers, Wheaton, Ill.

10 9 8 7 6 5 4 3 2 1

Dedication

To Verla, my wife, who has shared my dream of
building a caring-sharing community of
believers and has supported me in its pursuit;

To our children, Coleen, Joanne, Merrill, and Dale,
who through their demonstration of love and
cooperation have added to the joy of the
journey; and

To my mother, who through childhood training
helped produce the inspiration for my dream.

Contents

The Bible Speaks Clearly

"Pastor, the church I've been attending has some very fine people, and the pastor is a good man, but I haven't been able to find the kind of fellowship that I feel I need."

This comment has been heard literally scores of times as individuals and families have tried to explain why they chose to visit our church. Some of them eventually become integrated into the life of our congregation in an apparently satisfying relationship. Others have continued in their search for a church which would more adequately fulfill their needs. A few of these dissatisfied persons finally returned to the former church and found the contentment which had previously been lacking.

Pastors and laypersons in nearly every city, village, and rural community across the nation have observed people in a similar search. Though the characteristics of the area vary widely, and the people's names differ, there remains one common denominator. There is a hunger in the heart of every person for a loving-caring relationship with others.

Those of us who regard the Bible as our Sourcebook for truth should not be surprised at this quest. From the earliest written record of God's movements, we see God himself deriving satisfaction through fellowship with His creation. From time to time God demonstrated His disappointment when that fellowship was broken or disrupted.

On the sixth day of His great creative work, the Triune God said, "Let us make man in our image, after our likeness" (Gen. 1:26). This crowning act of God's creative work involved the creation of man who shared God's holiness and righteousness. Man in his original state fulfilled God's original purpose of a loving, willing fellowship.

As the Genesis account reveals "[Jehovah] God walking in the garden in the cool of the day" (3:8), we are led to believe that a very intimate fellowship had been enjoyed in daily visits within the Garden of Eden. Sin's intrusion into this beautiful setting marred the relationship and made fellowship on the previous high level impossible apart from God's remedial action. Thus God proceeded to effect His plan of redemption whereby man could be restored to fellowship.

Other personalities in the Old Testament account also are depicted as participants in a close fellowship with God. Enoch experienced such a close walk with God that he was taken to heaven so that their walk would remain uninterrupted (Gen. 5:24). When the wickedness of man became so great that a decision was made to destroy man from the face of the earth, the one chosen for deliverance from this severe judgment was Noah, whose walk with God was viewed acceptably (6:8-9).

In order to fulfill His intention for man's restoration and be able to experience fellowship with the whole human family, God chose a man who was identified as "the Friend of

God" (Jas. 2:23; cf. 2 Chron. 20:7; Isa. 41:8). Through God's friend, Abraham, a people was selected through whom He sought to bring the entire human family back to Him and His fellowship.

Repeatedly in God's dealings with Abraham's natural descendants, the children of Israel, there were promises of God's presence among them to assure them of His desire for fellowship with His people (Exod. 29:45; Lev. 26:12). Although there were frequent inclinations on the part of this people to forsake His true worship, God's mercy was manifested in an extensive measure as He sought to preserve the fellowship which He so highly cherished.

Fellowship Among Men

Although it is true that God derived satisfaction through fellowship with His creation, He also carefully planned for a satisfactory fellowship within the human family. Since man was created in His image, it would be normal for man to experience similar desires for companionship. Gen. 2:18 records this observation, "And the Lord God said, It is not good that the man should be alone."

Therefore, included in the Creator's grand design was the provision of a material being of his own kind for practical, physical, and spiritual companionship. It is noteworthy that man's mate was not created simultaneously but rather later and in a manner that produced the elements of dependency and support. "Her very body was dependent upon him for its existence, yet so designed as to supply that in which he was lacking."[1]

Not forgetting the need for harmonious relationships within the basic family unit, the Holy Scriptures abound with counsel and specific guidelines for family living. Careful adherence to these instructions enable the basic family to create an atmosphere where fellowship with God and His people is natural and normal. One might thus observe that the family is being encouraged to do modeling.

Christ and the Community

Jesus entering on the world scene through the Incarnation revealed yet another aspect of God's overriding concern for a satisfactory fellowship. Certainly we readily recognize that the ultimate purpose of Christ's first advent was to complete the redemptive plan, thus assuring the restoration of the fellowship marred by the disappointing response of man in the Garden of Eden. However, an important observation here is that Jesus placed great emphasis on the oneness or sense of community within the Church.

In Christ's great high-priestly prayer, His petition for the eleven who heard Him (John 17:11) and for the Church in general (vv. 21-23) was that the unity known in the Godhead would be their experience too. When the disciples of Jesus would experience the fellowship of the Spirit, the love which they possessed would produce a caring-sharing ministry that would influence others to believe in Christ. This kind of influence was seen as having the potential of spreading until Christ's redemptive purpose was shared around the world.

Underscoring His desire for oneness in the Body, Jesus offered a promise which assures us of His involvement. "Where two or three are gathered together in my name, there am I in the midst of them" (Matt. 18:20).

During the early days of the Church, Paul, writing to the Romans, reiterated the "oneness" concept first introduced by the Master: "So we, being many, are one body in Christ, and every one members one of another" (12:5). Immediately apparent here is the requirement that we be both dependent and dependable parts of the whole. Our ability to share depends on our having a share in the Spirit; conversely, our having a share in the Spirit leads to sharing.

Sensing an ever present danger of would-be disciples aligning themselves with a false fellowship, John in his First Epistle points out that our fellowship must be rooted and grounded in the Godhead (1 John 1:3, 6-7). There is a continuous need to "walk in the light" lest our fellowship with God and other members of the Body be broken.

To further amplify what the apostle was saying in regard to the origin and dynamic of the Christian fellowship, Willard Taylor describes this unique Christian society:

> This is more than a cooperative venture of men of common interests, highly religious as they might be. It is more than a congenial and loving society of persons responding to human needs. It is a happening, like Pentecost, brought about by the Holy Spirit, who by His presence infuses hearts with the life of the Son, and thereby creates a *koinonia.*[2]

Arising here may be the temptation to detach ourselves from any personal responsibility for furthering the sense of community, since our fellowship originates with the Father, and through His Spirit we are energized. Lest we view our personal endeavors to promote and preserve the fellowship of the Spirit as futile, we will do well to heed the injunction in Eph. 4:3-4, "Endeavouring to keep the unity of the Spirit in the bond of peace. There is one body, and one Spirit, even as ye are called in one hope of your calling." This word from Alex Deasley is instructive:

> The point of practical importance is that, while we cannot create the unity of the Church, we can destroy it; while we cannot make people participate in the Spirit, we can create conditions in which those who do participate express that fellowship for the good of the body of Christ with more rather than less difficulty.[3]

Koinonia

The Greeks had a word called *koinonia* which appears 18 times in the New Testament. A careful study of the word and its various usages indicates that it describes a relationship which is both vertical and horizontal. There is a fellowship between the Christian and God, between the Christian and other Christians, and each of these dimensions of fellowship are mutually dependent upon the other.

There has been a tendency to emphasize the vertical fellowship with the Spirit. However, James Reid, in his commentary on 2 Cor. 13:14, points out that the horizontal fellowship should perhaps receive primary attention:

> This does not mean fellowship with the Spirit. It is a fellowship with God which he shares through the indwelling Spirit with those who are members of the body of Christ. The fellowship of the Holy Spirit is the true description of the Church.[4]

Certainly we can agree that true koinonia must have its source in the Spirit. Then the expected consequence of this relationship with God through the Spirit is a oneness of purpose and common love for the brethren which fulfills Christ's prayer for the Church in John 17.

Practically, the expression of this anticipated fellowship within the body will be an acceptance of an obligation toward mutual responsibility. This is precisely what the apostle Paul was referring to when he wrote that through union with Christ as the Head, "the whole body, joined and held together by every supporting ligament, grows and builds itself up in love, as each part does its work" (Eph. 4:16, NIV).

Mutuality of Ministry

Identified in the New Testament Epistles are numerous instances where we are called to mutuality of ministry. Paul reminds us in Rom. 14:7 that "none of us liveth to himself, and no man dieth to himself." Our common love for the body results from God's manifestation within us which actively seeks the best interests of our brethren and does something for their needs.

In calling attention to the practical suggestions offered in the New Testament Epistles for mutuality of ministry within this caring-sharing community of believers, I mention seven areas. Admittedly this may not be an exhaustive list, but I feel these scriptural suggestions are at least basic to the building of a fellowship which creates the image of love God wants us to convey to our world.

1. *Mutual Acceptance*

> Wherefore receive ye one another, as Christ also received us to the glory of God (*Rom. 15:7*).

Our worldly society has created certain barriers which make it difficult for one to be accepted by those within a group where differences exist—racial, socioeconomic, cultural, etc. Unfortunately some of these same barriers have become bases for full acceptance within the church. Sometimes even additional barriers have been erected as legal requirements are imposed relative to specific areas of behavior and conduct.

One needs only to look to Christ's example of impartiality. He could always see more in people than others saw and could even see more than they were able to see in themselves. In spite of the scorn of the onlookers, Jesus said to Zaccheus, the most unpopular man of Jericho, "This day is salvation come to this house" (Luke 19:9).

Since we are brought to oneness in Christ, we must rise above differences. Differences as to position in life, cultural preferences, etc., will always exist, but before the Cross we are placed on the same plane.

2. *Mutual Prayer*

> Confess your faults one to another, and pray one for another, that ye may be healed (*Jas. 5:6*).

All of us hurt in different ways at different times, but we do hurt. It is at these times when we are hurting that we feel the need for the prayer support requested when healing is desired. Others cannot pray about our need unless they know what the need is. Bubna observes:

> Confessing our need to others shows our confidence in their love for us. It is acknowledging our mutual relationship of openness, acceptance, and trust.[5]

3. *Mutual Worship*

> Speaking to yourselves in psalms and hymns and spiritual songs, singing and making melody in your heart to the Lord *(Eph. 5:19)*.

Some would argue that the passage does not refer in any primary sense to public worship gatherings but rather to everyday social relationships. Not desirous of debating the issue, I would simply say that experience teaches us the highest form of worship occurs when the body gathers to express praise to God in psalms, hymns, and spiritual songs.

How often have we experienced those times when we came from our homes with heavy burdens which had made private conversation with the Lord difficult? There in the house of worship we were positively affected as we gathered with others of "like precious faith."

Kuhne, in his observations on worship, concludes, "Worship is meant to be a corporate activity. The sharing of praises, songs, thanksgivings, and prayers are the keys to worship."[6]

4. *Mutual Encouragement*

> And let us consider how we may spur one another on toward love and good deeds. Let us not give up meeting together, as some are in the habit of doing, but let us encourage one another—and all the more as you see the Day approaching *(Heb. 10:24-25, NIV)*.

Beyond the exhortation not to forsake the assembling of believers is the identification of one of the chief ministries we may perform while gathered with the body. Too often criticism and rebuke are practiced when the heart cry is for encouragement.

There is a responsibility resting upon the minister to give an encouraging word to the gathered worshipers even when the message takes on the nature of reproof. However, the task does not end with the preacher, for every participant in the worship experience is privileged to share in this mutual ministry of encouragement through testimony and personal greetings.

Donald L. Bubna, who has led his church into a practical encouragement ministry, declared:

> Expressing love to others not only builds them up, but also helps our self-esteem. As a church, our goal is to present every one of us mature and whole in Christ. . . . Encouragement along the way not only helps us to get where we're going, but to enjoy where we are.[7]

In the final phrase of the scripture reference is a reminder to exercise even greater diligence as the apostasy of the last days threatens to pull both us and our brethren into a state of indifference.

5. *Mutual Concern*

> But exhort one another daily, while it is called To day; lest any of you be hardened through the deceitfulness of sin *(Heb. 3:13).*

Resident in the first human family was one by the name of Cain who asked, "Am I my brother's keeper?" (Gen. 4:9). There is no place for this kind of social irresponsibility in the body of Christian believers. It is essential when we see our brethren being overtaken by the deceitfulness of sin, to call their attention to the danger and with tender affection remind them of the dreadful consequences.

Richard Taylor in his commentary writes:

> A strong sense of group responsibility is the mark of a healthy church. . . . There should be a deep tone of devotion and mutual concern permeating every gathering of believers, even so-called "social gatherings." . . . They should see to it that in every hour of fellowship,

whether at the table or in play or in home groups, something is included which will reinforce spiritual zeal and holy purpose.[8]

6. *Mutual Comfort*

> Praise be to the God and Father of our Lord Jesus Christ, the Father of compassion and the God of all comfort, who comforts us in all our troubles, so that we can comfort those in any trouble with the comfort we ourselves have received from God *(2 Cor. 1:3-4, NIV).*

Here is a great anthem of praise to the One who provides us comfort in the midst of life's troubles. As is always the case with praise, not only do we focus our attention on the infinite God, but invariably a response from us is called for as an act of the highest adoration.

"What shall I render unto the Lord for all his benefits toward me?" (Ps. 116:12). We discover that others of the Body of Christ are troubled, and we may comfort them with the same comfort He has given to us. What a golden opportunity to minister in time of need!

Lest we be inclined to complain because of the onslaught of suffering, we should be reminded that tenderness comes through suffering. Until we have suffered, we cannot sympathize. However, when others of the body observe our firmness in trouble made possible through the comfort of the Spirit, they in turn are comforted and strengthened.

7. *Mutual Sharing*

> Bear ye one another's burdens, and so fulfil the law of Christ *(Gal. 6:2).*

In the normal relationships of life, we all must share others' burdens to some degree. However, when this counsel is given to the Christian community, we are called upon to respond to the needs of others not just from the standpoint of hard necessity but in the spirit of Christian privilege.

A depth of sympathy is called for in Paul's admonition to

"rejoice with them that do rejoice, and weep with them that weep" (Rom. 12:15). But here we are asked to respond by taking an active role when others are seen carrying heavy loads. Going a step further, there may exist the thought that we are to be on the lookout for those in the body whose load has become too heavy.

The Early Church provided a vivid demonstration of this kind of burden bearing by sharing with the widows, the orphans, and the poor. Rarely does the church achieve this high level in our affluent age. Nevertheless, the scriptural suggestion is clear that this is our mutual ministry.

Throughout the Scriptures we readily perceive a biblical basis for the caring-sharing community of believers. In succeeding chapters we will be seeking to display those properties which seem to make the greatest contribution toward the building of this dynamic fellowship.

2

Guided by the Great Commission

"It is my firm conviction that if our church is to prosper and become the caring-sharing community of believers which God intended we should be, we must place a high priority upon the cause of world missions through practical involvement, fervent prayer, and sacrificial giving."

This statement of philosophy was being shared with my congregation near the conclusion of a Sunday morning service when we had just heard a challenging report from our visiting missionary. I had come only a few weeks before to serve as the pastor for this church which in its 20-year history had never seriously responded to the great missions challenge. During the previous church year barely over $1,000 had been given to missions out of a total annual budget of $37,000.

In the closing minutes of that Sunday morning service the people of that congregation signed faith-promise commitments for the next 12 months of world missions support for over $10,000. An electrifying atmosphere prevailed as scores of people took seriously the mandate of the Great Commission (Matt. 28:19-20).

Succeeding weeks of faith-promise giving to the great missionary enterprise of the church produced a new interest in the ongoing work of missions on fields both at home and abroad. Reports of victory and accomplishments brought forth an increased level of thanksgiving, whereas expressions of need produced an earnest prayer concern for our supported missionaries.

Not surprisingly, a new awareness of the responsibility of personal witness resulted during this same time period. There were numerous efforts in evangelism confrontation as well as a marked increase in ministering to one another within the body.

Way of Life

Frequently a church responding out of a sense of guilt seeks to put into practice a program of evangelism which doesn't necessarily reflect the everyday normal life of that congregation. Certainly we would not disagree with the need for intensified efforts toward evangelism approaches, but these emphases should not be isolated from the day-to-day expression of the church's focus of ministry.

Whenever a church recognizes that the Great Commission is valid for our day and time and proceeds to structure its ministry upon the basis of acceptance of the biblical command, it would be correct to expect that we will see evangelism becoming a way of life.

Paul S. Rees, in calling the church to a recognition of its potential, states, "There must be a sense of mission. This persuasion must be so strong that everything the church does is seen as having a bearing on its mission to the world."[1]

Whether structuring for worship, developing means of evangelism, arranging for fellowship opportunities, or suggesting ways for demonstration of concern, the church must be guided by a sense of evangelistic mission. Keeping this focus always before us will undoubtedly result in some necessary additions to and deletions from the church program. There is no excuse for a church-sponsored activity which fails to contribute to the fulfillment of the church's mission. On the other hand, every effort should be expended to do all possible to accomplish our mission.

While seeking to make evangelism a way of life, we must bear in mind that our Christian life-style as seen beyond the church walls needs to be consistent with our mission. No area of our lives, either secular or church-related, can be exempted from the requirement of demonstrating the Christian life-style. Anytime that our personal lives are out of alignment with our corporate life, there is a reduction in our organizational effectiveness.

Natural Witness

Too often we have attempted to program our people to share Christian witness when the basis for witness was not resident in the trainee. It is to this point that Shoemaker speaks, "If we are to make faith real to individuals, it must be real to us, and what we say of it must flow out of us as naturally as laughter or interest in our work."[2]

Certainly this is not to imply that we lessen our interest and involvement in training for effective soul winning, but we should strive to bring potential trainees to a level of Christian living where their witness becomes natural and free.

In referring to those in the church whose witness effectively contributes to church growth, McGavran comments, "Evangelism becomes their joy; it is a normal expression of their lives."[3]

We may well discover that the natural witness of one

whose Christian experience is real and vibrant and growing will often prove to be more effective than the skillful verbalization of the person trained to say all the right things in the right way.

Go Ye vs. Come

A major deterrent to a congregation being able to reach out in a caring-sharing ministry to others is the adoption of a philosophy which says, "We're here to serve you. Please come."

Without intending to restrict the growth of koinonia, the congregation with the "come" philosophy tends to become content with the fellowship of the present members of the body until natural mobility decreases the constituency. Only then do they become aware of the self-defeating nature of their approach to ministry.

Church growth is adversely affected when the congregation develops a strong satisfaction with the Sunday gatherings limited to the church building. The weekly gathering of the faithful in an all-too-familiar environment results in a smaller group and an atmosphere lacking in spiritual vitality because there has been no effort toward reproduction.

Common sense teaches us that our adherence to the scriptural mandate to "go ye" and add to the fellowship is a practical necessity. However, lest we be inclined to quickly whip up a program of saturation evangelism to find a quick cure for our ills, we need to remember that "true involvement can come only from internal motivation. The 'go ye' must be in the heart as well as in the head."[4]

The spiritual satisfaction of putting God's "go ye" formula into motion and the excitement of seeing new members in the body will literally transform the life of any congregation.

Limited Time

Most church members are familiar with the terms of the Great Commission from our Lord. Therefore, lack of awareness of responsibility is not the crucial problem.

Also we would propose that most of those in the church really intend to become involved in some way in following the Lord's command. However, the common enemy *procrastination* robs them of the privilege of participation in this essential task of the church.

Only as a sense of evangelistic mission grips us will we break loose from our state of lethargy and actively pursue the evangelization of the unsaved. We must move with all diligence and speed, for the time of opportunity is rapidly slipping from us.

Quoting pioneer missionary Robert Moffatt: "We shall have all eternity in which to celebrate our victories, but we have only one short hour before the sunset in which to *win* them."[5]

Congregational Responsibility

In an age of specialization when we are accustomed to securing someone to perform all needed services, often the church has yielded to the temptation to hire professionals to care for needed areas of ministry. Our lack of success in evangelism has proven this approach to be a failure.

If nothing else is considered apart from the sheer numbers of the unsaved to be reached, we must quickly come to the conclusion that dependence on a hired ministerial professional will be in vain. Paul Benjamin, in *The Growing Congregation*, observes that "only as the number of harvesters is dramatically increased can we begin to think of reaching a rapidly multiplying harvest."[6]

Of course, we know that even more important than the

magnitude of the task is the realization that all of us are responsible to God to carry out His plan. In spite of our fears or our efforts to shift responsibility to a paid church staff, the obligation is such that we cannot avoid the personal thrust of the Great Commission if we are serious about our commitment to Christ.

Perhaps our greatest need is to so saturate ourselves in the Word of God that we begin to sense the divine compassion and the importance of the task assigned to us. Kenneth Chafin states that "no church ever understands the heart of God until it sees Him reaching out to the unreached with a message of forgiveness and hope, and an invitation to discipleship of life."[7]

Direct Confrontation

There has been a time even in this century when the local body of believers could succeed to a degree in its outreach efforts by relying on mass evangelism. However, with the advent of modern transportation, television, and an abundance of entertainment possibilities, the old-time revival meeting or evangelistic crusade no longer is the fruitful method it used to be. Although there is still a place for the crusade approach today, we must hasten to say that it encourages a reliance on the "come" philosophy.

A study of churches which are building caring-sharing communities of believers reveals that the members of the body are actively confronting people with the claims of the gospel. Many of our neighbors and work associates will never come to our churches to listen to our cleverly worded sermons until first one of Christ's disciples has shared on a one-to-one basis the gospel presentation.

Arn insists that "there is a relationship between the amount of time and effort and the number of people involved in direct evangelism and the growth of the church."

He further suggests that greater success in direct evangelism is achieved when an effort is made to tailor an approach which is consistent with the personality of the church and the needs of the community to be reached.[8]

Not to be overlooked are the spiritual benefits which accrue to those who as a result of sharing their faith in direct confrontation experience the joy of making disciples. Nothing has greater potential for contributing to the experience of koinonia.

Training

Occasionally, we may observe a church which is so spiritually charged that many of its members are actively involved in direct evangelism without any special training. This is, however, not the norm. Most of us do not feel comfortable in a task for which we are poorly trained.

Therefore, the church which desires to measure up to the New Testament standard should seriously consider the implementation of an appropriate training program. A worthy goal is to bring every member into the training process so that all are equipped for the work of evangelism.

While the temptation will be present to seek to train all the members of the body through some mass effort, this must carefully be avoided. It is more fruitful to start with one or two so that actual on-the-job instruction is part of the training. When these are trained, they may join you as trainers and the multiplication process has begun.

An acquaintance of mine visited the Coral Ridge Presbyterian Church of Fort Lauderdale, Fla., which is noted for its extensive lay evangelism training program. He had been ushered to one of the few remaining seats just prior to the beginning of one of the morning services. Addressing himself to the person seated at his side, he asked the secret of the church's great success. His answer was, "Don't you know? We're all evangelists!"

Family Orientation

McGavran notes that "the pattern in the New Testament is not that of individuals one by one accepting the Lord; it is rather that of family by family."[9]

The observation by McGavran of this New Testament pattern could well serve as a warning signal relative to some outreach efforts which are not necessarily family oriented. Let there be no mistake. We do believe individuals are important in God's plan of salvation. Nevertheless, it seems that directing our efforts toward the winning of families would not only serve to accelerate soul winning but also provide for a built-in support system from the other members of the family unit.

One popular evangelistic ministry which has tended to ignore the family orientation is the bus ministry approach. Many congregations in an attempt to give a quick boost to attendance statistics have launched a full-scale bus ministry with emphasis on bringing children while making no provision for reaching the whole family unit. Some of these endeavors have continued for years with little or no permanent gains within the body, primarily because of improper orientation. In all fairness not all bus ministry efforts have followed this pattern but rather have made significant contributions to the body.

Promotion of family life crusades, establishment of Christian family life ministries, "each family win a family," and the bringing together of families into "Circles of Concern" all represent responsible attempts to bring families into the caring-sharing community of believers.

An acceptance of the responsibility for the Great Commission which results in a profound sense of evangelistic mission is destined to bring success to the combined efforts of the body. Benjamin suggests that "something wonderful usually happens when the members of a congregation begin systematically to seek the lost for Christ. People will respond."[10]

Recently a young lady in our congregation brought her friend to church following her conversion in a direct confrontation. Other members of the body had been prepared for her coming and were quick to demonstrate friendliness and personal interest. One of the older ladies was unable to contain her enthusiasm and proceeded to hug and kiss the new babe in Christ as she expressed personal joy for her newfound faith. The new convert was noticeably moved and was heard to say, "I can't believe how excited all of you are about what has happened to me. It's like I've always been part of your family."

"When the world sees Christians gathering in love and unity, it will stop and look."[11]

3

Welcome to Our Church

A warm July weekend found our family in a large midwestern city for a few days of vacation. On Sunday morning we decided to visit a church of our denomination which had been known as one of our great city churches.

Arriving at the church about 15 minutes before the announced time of the worship service, our family of six entered the foyer. Although we could hear distant sounds of voices in other parts of the building, there was no one in view. On a table nearby we observed some printed Sunday bulletins which we took to acquaint ourselves with what was happening. Then we entered the spacious sanctuary and seated ourselves.

The only greeting we would receive that morning came in the next few minutes as the people began coming into the sanctuary from their Sunday School classes. An elderly gentleman came down the aisle where we were seated and was shaking the hands of those who were gathering and voicing the comment, "Praise the Lord." I was one of those who received his handshake and his expression of praise.

There were perhaps 150 people assembled that morning in a sanctuary designed to seat hundreds. As it turned out, there were few people around us, so we tended to be highly visible. Yet no effort was made to determine our identity or to give us any kind of welcome.

During the service we learned that the church was experiencing a financial crisis, and a fund-raising drive was being launched that week. Some of the professional financial consultants were present that day and participated in the service.

When the service concluded, our family made our way back through the foyer and outside to our cars. No one made any effort to detain us and make us feel wanted. Admittedly, we were not prospects for their church, but they could not have known that. You can be certain if we had been searching for a church that our search would have taken us elsewhere.

As a churchman looking on, it was plainly obvious to me that this congregation had lost sight of its New Testament objective of reaching out to people in love and warmth of fellowship. Their financial crisis was only a symptom of the underlying cause of a dying church. As is so often the case in such situations, they were treating the symptom rather than giving attention to the basic cause.

Everyone Made to Feel Welcome

Contrary to what is sometimes viewed as the exclusive role of the greeters, the visitors are not the only ones coming through the church doors who need to receive a friendly word of welcome. When people emerge from their cars and walk across the parking lot to the church entrance, their emotional state may be at a desperate low. Struggles on the job, domestic strife in the home, and the feeling that they have poorly coped have marked their week. They could well afford to see a smiling face and hear a word of acceptance.

People in the church who have accepted the responsibilities of greeters or ushers stand in a unique position to offer expressions of a caring-sharing ministry where it is most needed. Leslie Parrott, in referring to this ministry, states that "a Spirit-directed word of encouragement, reassurance, or kindness may be the most significant ministry some people receive in their entire church attendance experience."[1]

Since everyone does not feel comfortable with this task because of a feeling of inadequacy, some form of preparation or training seems desirable.

Donald L. Bubna describes a program he has developed in his church which offers helpful insight. Each month 12 couples are chosen for placement at each entry to the church. To assure that all are met with a friendly greeting, greeters come 30 minutes early on the first Sunday of their duties for a training session which includes role playing of their assignment. Also a suggestion sheet is provided to give ideas for conversation starters.[2]

Though the ministry of greeting is beneficial to all gathering worshipers, the newcomer requires special consideration. For him there is a strangeness about the people, the building, and perhaps even the worship approach. Every effort needs to be made to eliminate as much as possible the feeling of strangeness.

Some growing churches begin their ministry of welcome in the parking lot. Attendants meet them at the parking lot entrance, extend a special welcome, direct them to the most convenient parking space, and then inform them where to enter the building. All of this has required a minimum of time and effort but has greatly helped to assure the newcomer that this church cares about him.

Certainly no church, regardless of size, should ever neglect having someone at the door to greet the newcomer and offer the help he needs in this new situation. Asking his name and other pertinent information not only makes a follow-up possible, but also indicates a personal interest. Most visitors will not object to supplying this information, but a few will, and care should be exercised not to offend by being too insistent.

The particular situation and building arrangement may suggest the need to give special help in getting to the place of meeting. Some buildings are so large or so designed as to make it difficult to know where to go for the worship service or other meeting occasion. Some churches provide a printed card showing a map of the building layout as well as a listing of the various events and the designated area for each. In addition to the printed card, signs giving directions are an indication of the thoughtful regard for the person who lacks familiarity.

In the case of families who have come for Sunday School or in instances where age-level church services are provided, there is the need to assist each family member in getting to the right place without his needing to hunt for it. This may be accomplished by introducing the guest to a regular attender and enlisting his help in taking the newcomer to the appropriate place. Also the greeter should make it clear to the person asked to escort the guest that he is to introduce the newcomer to someone in the area where he is being taken.

There are many conflicting ideas relative to the recognition of visitors within the worship service. In very large churches with an extensive list of guests, this may seem to be inadvisable. However, for the great majority of churches there should be some approach that would make such recognition a way of saying, "We're glad you've come."

Across the years I have discovered that many people dislike having the pastor call their names and asking them to stand. In recent months in our church one of our fine laypersons meets each guest before they enter the service. Then at a designated point in the service, that layman introduces each guest to the pastor from a microphone at the side of the platform. When the layman asks the person to stand in connection with the introduction, I detect less resistance to the request. The secret here is probably the employment of a layperson who has the capacity to make each guest feel important. We have been blessed at this point, and hopefully your church will be, too.

Of special concern is that the newcomer feels comfortable within the service. Since it is possible that the worship approach is unfamiliar, there is a need to provide some form of attachment. This may be accomplished when regular worshipers in response to their training arrange to sit with the person or persons and be prepared to assist as required.

With all our attempts to create an attitude of welcome through the use of effective human organization, there may exist certain barriers which negate many of our efforts—lack of provision for special needs of the handicapped, inadequate rest room facilities, poor sound quality, and a building facility which lacks in neatness and cleanliness. Some of these apparent barriers can be eliminated with a minimum of effort and expense. Others may require larger expenditures, but the dividends may be desirable.

Involving in Meaningful Fellowship

Recognizing that many visitors who come to our churches are looking for friendship, we need to be aware that many of the things we do in an attempt to create a welcome atmosphere may be regarded as only surface expression unless a deeper involvement is offered.

There are many churches who are so conscious of the need to involve newcomers in meaningful fellowship that plans are set in motion which will assure that no person or family leaves without an invitation to someone's home or an area restaurant for a meal or a snack, depending on the time of day. Efforts of this type are highly successful as evidenced by the testimonies of those who say they only planned to visit once but were hooked by the friendship offered in this kind of encounter.

Our church has recently joined a growing number of churches who provide a coffee fellowship following the church services. At this point we are only doing this on alternate Sunday evenings, but I have already detected that newcomers most readily respond to this activity. This only serves to confirm the fact that our guests may be reaching out for meaningful fellowship.

It should be remembered that a certain level of trust will need to be developed before our guests feel free to accept our invitations to special fellowship. Therefore, if the first offer is declined, we should be prepared to pursue these opportunities to reach out.

Follow-up of Newcomers

None of our efforts to make the newcomer feel welcome and comfortable within the church setting are wasted, but the special attention should not cease with the conclusion of the service and related events.

An impression of genuine concern can be further strengthened in the succeeding days by letters from the church office expressing appreciation for their visit and offering information about the church ministries. While sending these special mailing pieces, it would be profitable to add area visitors to the mailing list which would assure their receiving all regular mailings from the church.

Telephone calls and personal visits from members of the pastoral staff, Sunday School personnel, etc., produce a warm feeling in the hearts of those visitors who now know that this church and its people truly care about them.

Several years ago while I was serving as an associate pastor of a church in a large midwestern city, our family took a temporary leave one Sunday morning and visited a well-known church which had distinguished itself as one of the fastest-growing churches in America. Because of the distribution of ages within our family, we were able after the visitation experience to compare notes on what had happened in the Adult, Senior High, Junior High, Junior, and Primary departments.

However, our learning experience did not end with the visit itself. On Monday evening the youth pastor and teen president appeared at our door to express interest in our family. During the week there were letters and three separate phone calls designed to let us know we were wanted. Then on Saturday morning a visitor from the Adult Department stopped by our house for a visit. Needless to say, had we been looking for a church home, we would have been greatly affected by the caring-sharing ministry which was in evidence.

Perhaps a further word needs to be said about the continuing ministry of the church to newcomers which really becomes the most effective follow-up. MacNair says it well:

> There is a place for name cards for visitors and for "ice-breaker" programs for visitors, especially in the first few visits to the church; but these efforts must only begin, not constitute, the ways and means of fellowship. Actually, the "glad-handing" of a newcomer to church should only make it possible for him to see he is wanted and needed for himself and that the church has that which he needs. If the program of "ice-breaking" for new members does not lead to this conclusion within one or two months, the newcomer will probably be a dropout.[3]

Ongoing Ministry

The ministry of greeting worshipers and seeking to convey friendship and create a feeling of ease should not stop as long as the church seeks to fulfill its mission. This ongoing ministry provides an opportunity for consecrated greeters and ushers to cause those who come through the church doors to feel wanted.

Parrott calls attention to the value of this continuing ministry:

> The attitude the usher communicates to church members and friends helps set the tone for everything else which is to happen. As an official representative of the church of Jesus Christ, the usher has an enormous obligation in helping lead people into readiness for learning, worshiping, and evangelism. . . . The attitude the usher demonstrates in the foyer of the church is a forerunner to the ministry to be experienced in the sanctuary.[4]

All who are involved in this ministry will profit from a careful reading of the instruction given by the apostle in Jas. 2:1-9. There must always be constant attention given toward seeing people for themselves and not what their potential may seem to indicate from man's viewpoint.

Looking back over several years of pastoral service, I am grateful for a host of dedicated personnel who gave themselves to this vital ministry. Their faithfulness in using their God-given gifts further strengthened my effectiveness as their pastor.

A Turnaround

Ofttimes discouraged pastors and concerned laymen who recognize that their church is failing to demonstrate friendliness through the greeting process ask if a turnaround is possible.

Early in this chapter, a description of my family's visit to such a church was described. About seven years later we were vacationing for a few days prior to enrolling two of our children in college. Being in the same city and having heard that the church we had earlier visited had relocated and was experiencing growth under strong pastoral leadership, we decided to visit this church again.

This time the occasion was a Sunday evening service. Before we reached the entrance, someone opened the door for us and greeted us warmly. Inside the foyer three different persons extended a welcome and directed us to the guest register where we were asked to give our names and address. Then we were introduced to an usher who seated us. During the service we were recognized publicly. The vibrancy of the service seemed to say to us that this crowd had formed a new self-image and liked what they had become.

By the way, the pastor was the same one who served at the former location. Later we were to discover that on the occasion of our first visit, he had just recently arrived at the church. Over these years the pastor and people had decided to do something about their no-growth situation by treating the cause and had won.

"So, warmly welcome each other into the church, just as Christ has warmly welcomed you; then God will be glorified" (Rom. 15:7, TLB).

4

Is There a Group for Me?

"I'm looking for a church that is warm and loving—one where I can experience the fellowship that I feel I need."

This comment came from the lips of a young schoolteacher who had been introduced as a visitor in our service that morning. She had spoken to me as I greeted the worshipers exiting from the sanctuary. Although she expressed appreciation for the service, I had the distinct feeling we had not measured up to that for which she was looking. She did not return.

Perhaps she said it differently than others, but her real question that morning when she entered our church was, "Is there a group into which I would fit?"

Much has been written about those factors which contribute to the success of a church, such as favorable location, size of church, etc. Yet there is no factor more important in the mind of the prospect than his ability to fit in with the group.

Small-Group Methodology Not New

Recently much attention has been given to the dynamics of the small group. One might even presume that a new approach was being proposed. However, a study of church history soon reveals that small groups have been around for a long time.

In the scriptural record of the first-century church, we are told that "they, continuing daily with one accord in the temple, and breaking bread from house to house, did eat their meat with gladness and singleness of heart" (Acts 2:46). These early Christians spent their time in two distinct areas—congregational worship and small groups.

The early Methodists under John Wesley employed a small-group strategy known as the class meeting. There was a sense of togetherness and mutual support within this group as well as the recognized obligations of accountability.

During my own childhood days I remember that the cottage prayer meeting was employed with great profit. As we met in individual homes for prayer, praise, and Bible study, unchurched people often were invited and eventually were won to the fellowship of the church. It is possible that some of these thus won would not have been reached through the larger congregational structure. Also those of the church who participated in these small-group sessions were experiencing satisfaction as their own fellowship needs were met.

Dynamics of the Small Group

In describing his congregation's search for a method which would allow their people to share Christ's love with one another, Robert C. Girard indicates that small groups were chosen as the means which seemed most natural and effective. He stated that small groups "seemed the kind of structure which would allow the Holy Spirit the most freedom to do what He wanted to do in and through the body."[1]

Few of us are willing to bare our weaknesses, hurts, and failures with those we have not come to know well. In the gatherings of the total congregation we are inclined to hide under a facade. However, in the small group we are privileged to identify with others in a closer relationship and participate with them in a caring-sharing ministry to each other. Arn states that since the participants in the small group have come to know the others at "deeper levels," they "feel a freedom to be honest, to remove the masks, to be themselves."[2]

One of the most frequent employments of the small group is what has commonly come to be known as prayer cells. Many Christians could testify to the fact that some of their most rewarding experiences in prayer resulted from participation in a prayer cell.

Not uncommonly, prayer tends to be general in nature. How often we have heard a petition offered for the missionaries who serve on foreign soil. There is really no concrete identification with any particular missionary. Within the context of the prayer cell, specific persons and situations are the objects of prayer. Because these objects touch our lives, the prayer experience becomes much more meaningful.

There is no question in the minds of those who have tried it that there is a great power resident in the small group if the concept is properly used. Those who are seeking to build a caring-sharing community of believers will most certainly want to tap this productive resource.

Homogeneous Principle

Church growth studies always arrive at the conclusion that there is a homogeneous principle which determines the degree of success a church experiences when it seeks to minister to people of differing backgrounds and interests.

Though it may occasion some embarrassment to admit this fact in light of what we believe the gospel of Jesus Christ is able to accomplish, the fact must be reckoned with in all our efforts. This has particular significance in setting up any structure for small groups.

It has been my privilege in pastoral labor to serve a broad spectrum of people representing many different socio-economic levels. My observation has been that within the context of the Christian Church those at higher levels, by worldly standards, seek to break down the barriers. However, those at lower levels find it difficult to relate, and thus a chasm exists in spite of our efforts.

One young professional couple related their experience with an involvement in their local church when they were assigned to a small group for fellowship purposes. The organization of these small groups was so designed that most of their fellowship was necessarily limited to this group. In the spirit of true loyalty they tried to cooperate but became greatly discouraged since they had nothing in common with other members of the group. They even considered leaving the church to escape the unpleasant situation.

A very careful analysis of social circumstances such as occupation, income, family, and interest should be considered in the composition of the small groups. Grouping on the basis of the homogeneous principle will assure the greatest success.

Emphasizing the Individual

On any given Sunday in most churches there are those worshipers who feel a lack of importance, unneeded, and unwanted. When the ministry of the church is largely limited to the congregational gatherings, the likelihood exists that this feeling will continue.

Much of the small-group concept lies in the opportunity it provides to focus attention on the individual and allow him to regain a measure of self-worth. Benjamin notes that "a congregation which emphasizes small study groups in homes often has renewed interest in worship on Sunday morning." He further comments that "in an age of depersonalization, it is imperative that the congregation keep its emphasis upon the individual."[3]

There is a great need on the part of every member of the body to feel that he is desired within the group for his own sake and not just for what he may be able to contribute. Selfishness and greed have caused some persons within the church to use others for selfish ends. However, proper utilization of the small group makes possible a proper ministry to the individual. Howard A. Snyder, in *The Problem of Wine Skins*, quotes Elton Trueblood:

> When a person is drawn into a little circle, devoted to prayer and to deep sharing of spiritual resources, he is well aware that he is welcome for his own sake, since the small group has no budget, no officers concerned with the success of their administration, and nothing to promote.[4]

The small group may serve to keep the one individual from getting lost in the bigness of the total congregation.

Importance of Early Involvement

In his book which discusses ways in which new members may be brought into the life of the body, Lyle E. Schaller makes this observation: "Adult new members who do not become part of a group, accept a leadership role, or become involved in a task during their first year tend to become inactive."[5]

For those of us who are concerned with the building of a caring-sharing community of believers, this revelation is very disturbing. Potentially, all our gains could be wiped out unless proper steps are taken to insure early involvement of new members.

Traditionally church nominating committees have been hesitant to place new members in leadership roles during their first year. Particularly is this true if the new member has come into the body through a new profession of faith rather than transfer from another congregation. The committee's reluctance at this point is not only due to reservation about the person's ability to perform, also there is a special regard for the spiritual welfare of the new member lest the assignment should prove to be hurtful at a time when he is still spiritually immature.

Involvement in a task may be feasible, but often the new member waits until he has become better acquainted with the people and expected ways of doing things before committing himself to any continuing involvement.

Is there any reason why the new member may not become part of a small group? On the contrary, there is every reason to believe that he should. His feeling of truly belonging may depend upon it. Therefore, wise church leaders will proceed with all haste to assure that this occurs.

Insiders Reaching Out

When outsiders come asking the question, "Is there a group for me?" they must await the final answer from the insiders. As insiders we are so prone to become content with the relationships we already enjoy and thus ignore the crying needs of the outsiders.

Kuhne provides a graphic description of the composition of the body which gives rise to the question posed by the outsiders:

<blockquote>
Experientially, the body of believers is made of a complex web of relationships. . . . Only when those inside the body go out of their way to build relationships with those outside and assist them in establishing additional relationships with others in the web will new Christians be able to become part of the body and benefit from what it can offer.[6]
</blockquote>

Meeting this outreach requirement will necessitate a concerted effort on the part of the insiders. Not only is it important to woo them in, but considerable attention must be given to creating an atmosphere where they feel a sense of belonging.

Our reaching out as insiders to outsiders will imply vulnerability. Nevertheless, our role as Christians requires that we be willing to take risks for Christ's sake. The Christian message says, "I am my brother's keeper." We must not take the time or waste the effort to count the cost.

Hopefully, our desire to build a caring-sharing community of believers will be so strong that we will demonstrate concern by taking whatever risks are required to reach out to the outsiders and build relationships.

Multiplication

To any person concerned with building a caring-sharing community of believers, the very mention of multiplication should bring an enthusiastic response. Too long we have been content to build the church by simple additions. Why not in the spirit of the Early Church move into a program of multiplication!

Webber addresses this exciting possibility:

<blockquote>
When the whole life of the congregation depends upon the minister, the resources are far more limited than when a congregation is made up of cells whose members have come to know one another in depth and who for
</blockquote>

each other release the sources of God's love. The possibilities are instantly multiplied.[7]

About six years ago a pastor friend of mine told me that there were more than 40 home Bible studies being conducted in the homes of his constituent families each week. These home Bible studies had come into being through a process of rapid multiplication during the few months prior to this information being shared with me. It was my friend's firm conviction that as these small groups met for Bible study and prayer and permitted the Holy Spirit to minister to them, the natural result would be both spiritual and numerical growth.

It would be the height of folly to suggest that the use of the small-group concept was the only factor contributing to phenomenal growth in this church. However, it would be just as foolish to overlook the tremendous impact of these small groups as this church has experienced a 150 percent increase in these last six years. Faster growth will probably occur when a church puts into motion a plan which allows for multiplication of fellowship groups.

Fellowship Experiments

There are probably few pastors who have not given considerable time and attention to the development of techniques which would encourage an active fellowship opportunity for everyone who comes. Since many of us feel inadequate in creativity, we often attempt to duplicate a procedure that has reportedly worked for someone else. Certainly there is nothing wrong with experimentation of this type, but it frequently results in disappointment, for what worked in another situation may not work for us.

Also it should be remembered that simply setting up a structure is insufficient. There must be a basis for fellowship. Webber comments: "You cannot create Koinonia. The fellowship of the church is a gift of God. God gives one the grace to love another person; one cannot, by gritting his teeth, determine to do so."[8]

Nevertheless, if we are convinced that a basis for true fellowship exists, it is not inappropriate to offer organized procedures by which this fellowship may function in an effective manner. If we are successful in implementing a workable plan, we may be in a definite minority, for Snyder contends that "the average church has no normative structure for true sharing and fellowship."[9]

The lack of structure could be a healthy situation if koinonia is so much in evidence that fellowship opportunities are naturally developing and everyone is being included in a group. However, the normal situation is that some are being excluded, though not by design, unless some standard plan is made available.

Numerous plans have received widespread attention. Some are so complicated that extensive bookkeeping and supervision are required. An exception is found in this simple program described by Orville W. Jenkins:

> In one church where there was a lack of genuine friendliness and fellowship, a plan was devised which enlisted the co-operation of all the families in the church. The plan was simple.
>
> Each family in the church was numbered, beginning with number one. Then the name of each family with its corresponding number was placed on a large placard in the vestibule of the church.
>
> The family numbers were placed on small cards. Once each month one of these numbers was drawn. After a number was drawn it was destroyed to avoid future duplication.
>
> Each family would add the number drawn to their family number. To illustrate, Mr. and Mrs. Brown, family number 4, would add 7, the number drawn, and the number 11 would indicate that they would invite Mr. and Mrs. David Cook to their home during the month for dinner and fellowship.

Family Name	Family Number	Number for the Month [7]	Your Family for the Month
CHURCH FAMILIES			
Mr. & Mrs. James Smith	1		8
Mr. & Mrs. Jim Jones	2		9
Mr. & Mrs. John Edwards	3		10
Mr. & Mrs. Robert Brown	4		11
Mr. & Mrs. Lee Simpson	5		12
Mr. & Mrs. Paul Mills	6		13
Mr. & Mrs. Leon Cook	7		14
Mr. & Mrs. Ralph Hall	8		15
Mr. & Mrs. Henry Cook	9		1
Mr. & Mrs. Edward Rowe	10		2
Mr. & Mrs. David Cook	11		3
Mr. & Mrs. Earl Lee	12		4
Mr. & Mrs. Herbert Green	13		5
Mr. & Mrs. George Bobbett	14		6
Mr. & Mrs. Jack Jenkins	15		7

When the total of the family number plus the number for the month was greater than the number of participating families, then one would subtract the number of participating families to get the identifying family number. To illustrate: Mr. and Mrs. Herbert Green, family number 13, would add 7 (number drawn) and get 20. Since 20 is greater than the number of families participating, they would subtract 15 (number of participating families) to get 5, the number of the family they would entertain.

In this way this pastor and his church families visited in each other's homes and soon that church became friendly, not only visiting among themselves, but also reaching outside to many unsaved homes.[10]

In one church I served we put the above described plan in motion, except that we included only those families who chose to participate after the plan had been presented. Furthermore, we requested that participating families be alert to new families attending the Sunday services and invite them to share in the month's planned fellowship.

The results were most encouraging as some longtime insiders shared in each other's homes for the first time. Also their reaching out to the outsiders produced a positive effect.

Many churches have used some variation of a plan called "Circles of Concern." Some report great success, whereas others end up in the junk heap of programs which started with lots of potential but died anyway. Could it be that we are only promoting a plan without seeking to clearly identify the purpose?

Too many people, including both long-time insiders and newcomers, come to our services and leave with a feeling of loneliness. Any plan for fellowship should have as its ultimate purpose the determination to reach out to others in such a way as to make them feel a part of the caring-sharing community of believers.

We do not need to be afraid of experimentation with fellowship plans if we are certain that a basis for fellowship truly exists. Can we afford not to experiment until we are certain that there is a group for everyone?

5

Needs, Needs, Needs!

Considerable debate has centered around whether the church should approach its task with a Bible-centered ministry or a need-centered ministry. Ultimately the controversy seems to come down to a matter of semantics. If a church concludes that its ministry shall be Bible-centered, a serious effort to effect a practical application must certainly focus on needs. On the other hand, the conclusion that its ministry is to be need-centered demands intense dependence upon the Bible to give answers which these needs require.

No discussion is necessary to determine if there are needs to which we should address ourselves. All who come within our sphere of influence have needs. It is not a question of "If," but rather, "How" shall we effectively confront these areas of need?

Basically, the great variety of needs which are recognized within our responsibility area fall into one of two general categories. There is a need to be ministered to and also a need to minister. To be true to its calling, the church which seeks to build a caring-sharing community of believers cannot ignore either of these pressing concerns.

Beyond the fact that any truly caring church will be desirous of meeting people's identified needs, there is the painful reminder that our ability to continue any kind of effective ministry requires a keen sensitivity to the needs of those we serve.

Experience has taught us that people are anxious to be identified with a church that meets their needs. We have also witnessed drop-outs and the departure of members to other churches when their needs were no longer fulfilled.

Many of us have identified individuals in their search for a church where possibly the answer to a deep-seated need could be found. Some of these searchers allow that church little time to respond to their need. They may in their initial visit conclude that a response is not forthcoming and therefore continue their search. Others may concede that the prospective need supplier is entitled to more than one chance, but eventually the church is judged as to its ability to meet them at the point of need.

A heartbreaking moment comes when a member of the body feels compelled to say, "I'm leaving the church because I no longer feel it's meeting my needs." Though there may be occasions when this statement is only an excuse to mask the true motive, too often it honestly exposes the church as to its failure to relate.

The implications are clear. If we are to reach new people and be able to add them to the body, a conscious attempt must be made to demonstrate an active concern as early as possible. Furthermore, there is no opportunity for coasting in the performance of our task. Unfortunately, the surfacing of needs knows no vacation. Thus we must be ready to respond whenever the concern is revealed.

Responding to Individual Differences

One of the greatest mistakes churches make is to determine a felt area of need and then focus all their energies upon that one area. In these situations it has been incorrectly assumed that what appears to be a predominant concern is shared by all.

Let us not err at the point of placing everyone in the same mold. Our people are different and our growth depends on an appropriate response to these differences.

There is a temptation to conclude that our time is too limited and valuable to provide a special ministry for only a few. Furthermore the matter of financial economics directs us toward a broader approach. It is at this point that the Holy Spirit flashes warning signals before us. "Is not one soul of greater value than the whole world?"

Instead of individualized ministry limiting our effectiveness, often a church has discovered an entirely new opportunity opening up to them because the individual has been given priority consideration. Chafin notes that "many churches have established an effective ministry with groups they had been unable to reach by first meeting some obvious need in the life of the person."[1]

Some small churches always have and probably will continue to fill a vital role in the lives of many families, but their very size places limitations on their ability to minister to many segments of society. Lack of money, personnel, and facilities automatically rule out some forms of ministry. Thus, responding to individual differences becomes a very frustrating task for the church which sees great needs but has few resources.

Though some would argue that there is a proper place for the small church, I believe we must realistically determine whether there is a minimal size which will allow appropriate response to people's individual needs. When evaluating growing churches in an attempt to determine their primary strengths, one trait which seems to surface is that they are of sufficient size to offer a broad spectrum of ministries to provide for the needs of their constituency.

Chaney and Lewis suggest that when the church considers diversified ministries, the following deserve our careful appraisal: "felt need in the community, gifts to perform that ministry, open doors, and program flexibility."[2]

Priority Consideration

While we readily recognize that the small church has a limited opportunity to minister to a wide variety of needs, we must also remember that comparatively few churches will achieve the "superchurch" status which allows for a seemingly unlimited scope of ministry. Therefore, priority consideration as to necessary services becomes a matter of prime importance.

Schaller and Tidwell in their book dealing with creative methods of administration remind us that "there are many good things a church might do—but there are comparatively few things a church must do."[3]

While pastors and laymen dream and numerous boards, committees, and task forces participate in brainstorming sessions, there must come that moment of truth when we honestly analyze our own situation and seek to do as much as is required and practical. Practicality forces us to take into consideration "what needs to be done, in order of priority, and then what resources, including money, we will need to do these things."[4]

There are some ministries that the average church will discover are not immediately practical even though the need is great. Our inadequacy of money and personnel to minister to certain need areas may force us to look for alternate means. The result may be surprising as we discover possibilities which we did not know existed.

A word of caution is in order when we are convinced that the need absolutely requires our response, but there seems to be no human way to act due to obvious barriers. Jesus declared, "If ye have faith as a grain of mustard seed, ye shall say unto this mountain, Remove hence to yonder place; and it shall remove; and nothing shall be impossible unto you" (Matt. 17:20).

Our Great Resource

Commonly offered excuses when statistics are decreasing and services are not performed revolve around professed lack of personnel. We have come to rely so heavily upon paid staff that we have overlooked our great resource. Chafin sounds an optimistic note:

> The discovery of the laity as the church's greatest resource for ministry is the greatest discovery of this day. These churches which have decided that they really want to do something for God and for the people have discovered talent, interest, and a commitment far beyond their expectation. The hope of the ministering church is the informed, inspired, committed layman.[5]

Some of our church members are actually waiting to be recruited while we are decrying the unwillingness of our laity to become involved in some form of ministry. Not long ago a pastor called one of his parishioners to request the performance of a special task thinking that a selling job would be required. However, when the request was made, the layperson responded, "I'll be happy to do it. In fact, I've been praying that God would provide some kind of ministry in which I could serve my church."

One cannot help but wonder how many laypersons are not involved because the church has overlooked their potential service. Furthermore, we are, of necessity, concerned about the vast numbers of needs for which no ministry is provided because we have failed to properly mobilize our forces.

Michael Green observes that "there is no suggestion in the New Testament that one could possibly be a Christian without having a call to some form of ministry within the church."[6] We have commonly referred to the divine call of those who give themselves to full-time service, but we have tended to neglect the aspect of a call for the individual layperson. Just the thought of our laity becoming totally involved in answering a divine call to some form of ministry raises some exciting possibilities.

Bringing laypersons into meaningful service necessitates our looking at the total structure of their lives. "The layperson has what is known as a double vocation," states Garlow. "He has a churchly ministry and a vocational ministry. Both must be included in order to have a balanced understanding of lay ministry."[7]

Our success in equipping the laity to adequately fulfill their "double vocation" could enable the caring-sharing community of believers to reach out into every avenue of life with phenomenal success.

Excitement of Involvement

Not only does the laity represent our greatest resource for ministry to others with needs, but an involved laity ultimately are fulfilling a basic need within themselves to minister. The layperson who is involved in ministry becomes excited about what God is doing in him and thus feels better about himself. With an improved self-image, he then is even more effective in ministry.

Frank was a relatively new Christian whom I was training in personal evangelism. In the particular home to which we had gone that night, the man of the house was only mildly receptive. As yet my young trainee was not confident enough about the step-by-step outline to give the gospel presentation, but he could share what God had done for him when he was saved out of a life of sinfulness. At a certain point in the interview, I asked Frank to relate his personal testimony. With eager enthusiasm he told about God's saving power which he had experienced and the wondrous change it had made in his life. Before our very eyes we saw evident hostility melting as Frank's testimony made an impact. When we left the house that night, Frank was literally throbbing with excitement because he had been able to minister, and that ministry had been effective.

Building a caring-sharing community of believers requires that many people begin to experience the excitement of involvement. Whenever a large concentration of people in a local church get excited about the potential of service for God and begin offering themselves and their assets, progress is almost certain to occur.

Special Ministries

If we are serious about providing a ministry which responds to people's needs, we cannot be content with the structured worship services as our only approach. Additional ministries must be brought into existence which take us outside our church buildings and into the community where the word of reconciliation is so desperately needed.

A recognition that traditional approaches are not sufficient leads us to seek for and experiment with different kinds of special ministries which can make a positive impact upon people with needs. John B. Nielson gives this explanatory statement:

> Special ministries are more than a response to the cultural orientation of our day. They are rather an awareness, by the religious community, that the needs of peo-

ple must be met on a more intimate level than is usually done through traditional functions. It is the conviction that, indeed, some persons will never be drawn into the full fellowship of the church until and unless they are first introduced to a need-meeting "subgroup." The validity for all these special ministries is that they meet needs on a level not readily attainable in "regular services."[8]

There is a great variety of special ministries which growing churches have employed. Selection of these special ministries must begin with the identifiable needs of the constituent community. There may be youth struggling with identity problems, parents without partners who are grasping for some kind of support system, singles who are plagued by loneliness, aged who feel forgotten, etc. Once the needs are identified, don't be afraid to enter into a program which provides for special ministries addressed to these need areas. Some of our special ministries will be less successful than others, but it will be better to be faulted for lack of perfection than for failure to try.

Charlie Shedd describes a program in his church in which over 250 people are called "undershepherds." These special lay ministers are involved in a prayer emphasis which commits them to pray daily for one to four families. Although the program is structured, it allows for flexibility in that the undershepherd decides how many families will be a part of his official prayer concern. The result has been a meeting of needs on many fronts, for real prayer leads us to demonstrate that we care in practical ways.[9]

A simple little procedure, an encouragement card, has been employed in Donald Bubna's church. Worshipers are asked following the sermon "to think of someone who needs a lift and write a few words of appreciation and love on the card."[10] On Tuesday, the office workers mail out the cards. This special ministry crosses over age barriers and effectively ministers to a wide variety of needs.

Extensive Structure Not Essential

Perhaps the most successful and effective efforts toward ministering to needs are those which are unentangled by organizational structure. When a congregation becomes a caring-sharing community of believers, expression of love and concern begins to flow naturally. Members of the body discover ways of ministering which fit them, and the efforts are blessed by the Holy Spirit.

A few weeks ago my wife, in response to an act of kindness by one of our church members, prepared a parchment copy of a poem done in calligraphy. Soon thereafter the following note was received:

> My dear Verla,
>
> What a delightful friend you are! I treasure your gift. How can I ever thank you?
>
> I thought—what can I ever do for Verla—so gifted, while I am so inept? And I realized that perhaps the one thing I already do is the best—I pray. I pray for your health, and your sleep, and your job, and your dear family, and your safety on the road, and strength for the day. I'm sort of a silent prayer partner.
>
> If it helps at all, I say, Praise the Lord!
>
> Love,
> PAT

The person who wrote this letter is certainly not inept, as she so humbly suggested, but rather is effectively communicating love. In her beautiful, quiet way she has developed a ministry.

6

Ready to Give an Answer

Indoctrination

Twice in one week members of two different cultist groups had called at the home of one of our newest Christians as a part of their missionary activity. My friend who had so recently experienced the joy of salvation had no doubt about the validity of his experience but was nevertheless somewhat overwhelmed by the heavy approach of these visitors.

When my phone rang that evening, the new Christian said, "Pastor, I need help. These people are confusing me. They quote scripture for everything they teach, and they're very convincing. I don't know how to answer them."

It was at this point in my pastoral ministry that I began to sense the tremendous importance of indoctrinating the members of the body with basic tenets of the faith. In many and varying circumstances they would find it necessary to provide answers to questions about their Christian faith. A Christian possesses a natural desire to share what God has done for him but is inclined to hold back if he is unsure of his basic beliefs. Even the full expression of Christian love is hindered when uncertainty in doctrinal matters produces a hesitancy in verbal witness.

Belief in Inspiration of the Scriptures

Building a strong foundation of Christian doctrine requires absolute dependence upon biblical understandings. However, using the Bible as the Textbook is of no value for indoctrination unless it is accepted as the inspired Word of God. Therefore, our first task centers upon bringing our people to a firm acceptance of scriptural inspiration.

Popular schools of religious thought suggest that the Bible contains the writings of some deeply religious men who have given us helpful thoughts which are useful as suggested guidelines. Some modern religionists concede that the Bible contains the Word of God in certain instances but stop short of accepting total inspiration. Any position which fails to receive the Bible as the verbally inspired, infallible Word of God is unacceptable as we seek to make disciples.

A proper understanding of scriptural inspiration enables us to see that the Bible does not just contain the Word of God, but rather it is the Word of God. Acceptance of this fact is basic to all of Christian doctrine.

With scriptural inspiration as a foundation, our efforts to indoctrinate by using biblical references take on tremendous significance. Bible truths fastened in the mind and treasured in the heart become the source of assurance for Christian experience and confidence in sharing our faith with others.

Adherence to the belief that the entire Bible is divinely inspired enables us to quickly gain an advantage over the cultists' efforts. This is true because we have no need to depend upon proof texts in isolation from other passages. Our confidence in the inspiration of the Scriptures frees us to study all of the Bible without fear of contradiction. Studying and acquainting ourselves with the entire Bible helps us to understand what the Bible is saying because we have come to recognize God's design for the world throughout all ages.

In our efforts to build the church, we will be strongly

influenced by conversation with other members of the body, literature designed for Christian education, and secular attitudes of the day. Lest these influences should at any point lead us in the wrong direction, we must resolve to be a people of "one Book." Though this is certainly not to suggest that we ignore the presence of other helpful assistance, it does say that we regard this "one Book" of such divine authority that all else must come under its scrutiny.

Togetherness in Testimony

Paul the apostle, in writing to the Corinthian brethren, called for togetherness in the matter of Christian testimony. "Now I beseech you, brethren, by the name of our Lord Jesus Christ, that ye all speak the same thing" (1 Cor. 1:10).

Divisions had characterized this first-century church. There was a lack of unity in the matter of their expression of belief. God was not glorified, and the influence of the church was producing a negative effect as a lack of unity prevailed.

Building a caring-sharing community of believers demands that there be a unity as to the basics of Christian doctrine. Unity serves to strengthen the fellowship, whereas disunity creates division and disrupts the sense of koinonia. James Earl Massey expresses his conviction:

> Togetherness in belief serves to preserve togetherness in behavior. Fellowship includes and involves what a man believes. And where clarity is lacking, there will be much confusion and a vacuum for evil work.[1]

Particularly it is important for new Christians coming into the fellowship of the body to be able to hear the same expressions of belief coming from all. In their elementary stage of Christian experience, hearing conflicting sounds may retard growth and hinder the progress toward maturity. Uncertainty in the expression of our beliefs makes it nearly impossible for the new convert to gain sufficient trust to become a part of any close, intimate fellowship within the body.

Any lack of togetherness in our testimony certainly decreases our ability to reach out in evangelistic endeavor and bring new members inside. When the new members are not being brought in, excitement wanes and the present members become discouraged, inactive, and perhaps even leave.

When the members of the body are well versed in the church's beliefs and doctrine and are "speaking the same thing," the resultant unity and harmony become attractive to the outsider who seeks for spiritual reality based on certainty. His coming inside causes excitement to mount within the body, and the building of a caring-sharing community of believers moves forward with great momentum.

Investing Our Lives in Others

The task of indoctrination in the work of building a caring-sharing community of believers provides a splendid opportunity for those who are strong in the faith to render valuable service. As those strong in the faith look back to their spiritual beginnings, they will recall many incidents where weaknesses forced them to depend on God, trials faced in the power of the Spirit brought them to a new level of spiritual victory, insights were gained as God was observed working out His purpose in their lives. These experiences ought to be shared and will greatly profit those who are new in their spiritual pilgrimage.

MacNair expands on the scriptural admonition when he declares that "mature members of the church . . . should spend the time and love necessary to appreciate every young babe in Christ and give each one personal encouragement, insights, challenges, exhortations, etc. (I Corinthians 12:12)."[2]

This concept of sharing in the work of indoctrination may be regarded as a matter of investing. By pouring their lives into newer members of the body, an investment of eternal proportions is being made. There is no way to calculate what the returns may be when seasoned Christians allow the Holy Spirit to work through them as they invest their lives in others.

Two specific benefits may be readily observed. First, the weaker Christian forms an attachment to the body which tells him he is valuable to the group or else he would not be given the attention he has received. When trials come and pressures mount, there is special incentive to succeed, for he dares not disappoint the body. Also he recognizes that he can count on others in the body to give mutual support and encouragement.

The second benefit comes to the investor. There is no greater satisfaction to us as children of God than to see growth and development occurring in the life of a brother or sister to whom we have contributed as God has enabled us. Eventually, we may even see this one into whose life we have poured ourselves make a similar investment in others, and we thus have set in motion a process of spiritual multiplication.

Equipping Through the Sunday School

Although the Sunday School has been around for more than 200 years and some are suggesting that it will eventually die, there is strong reason to believe that it is still the most effective means available to us to equip the greatest number of people for ministry. Its past successes suggest that we should not ignore the great potential which it offers us today.

Unquestionably, in many places the Sunday School has come to be no more than an institution. Where purpose is lacking, such an organization will be nonproductive. However, such does not need to be the case. Stedman, in his description of "body life," provides us a view of the Sunday School as it ought to be:

> Our entire Sunday School is set up to equip the saints, of all ages, to do the work of the ministry. The work of expounding and applying the Scriptures begins with the pulpit and is continued in every class, in every gathering, and in many of the homes of Christians.[3]

Due to the fact that the Sunday School has gained such wide acceptance, its very credibility commends it to us as one of the most advantageous organizational structures available for an equipping ministry. Though I wouldn't suggest that the Sunday School offers the only answer, I believe wisdom says we should seek to avail ourselves of all the benefits it potentially holds out for us in equipping our people with answers to life's questions.

A historical perspective of the past periods of dynamic growth in our churches reveals that the Sunday School has made a significant contribution. The implications are clear. The Sunday School has served us well in a period of aggressive church growth. We would thus be well advised to take steps to employ this time-tested organization in such a way as to gain maximum benefits in equipping the church for ministry.

Expanding Christian Education

While defending the maximum employment of the Sunday School as a valid strategy, I must hasten to declare that further steps need to be taken to adequately equip our people to function as healthy Christians in today's complex world. The Sunday School has been a faithful servant, but far too many of the body are yet ill-equipped.

Getz speaks to the serious gap in doctrinal understanding in the following statement:

> Unfortunately, there are individuals in the twentieth century church who have been Christians for years, but

who have never been taught even the most elementary
Bible doctrines. It is here we must begin in the edification
process, whether we are ministering to "new babes" or
"old ones."[4]

An increasingly popular method used in the expansion
of Christian education is the program of discipling. In my
own church, I have discovered this to be an acceptable approach for bringing new Christians together with veterans of
the faith as we seek to study Christian doctrine in an informal
classroom setting. This course of instruction takes us from
elementary doctrines on to more complex doctrinal study. An
effort is made to bring all to an understanding of principles of
Bible doctrine which will give a firm basis for their faith in
every situation in life.

In the discipling classes, opportunity is provided to share
with the smaller group the ways God has been using us as
His disciples and the specific needs which have been identified in our Christian journey. This kind of open sharing coupled with doctrinal instruction provides an atmosphere
favorable for true koinonia.

Home Bible studies mentioned in an earlier chapter also
offer another possible expansion of the church's educational
program. There are literally hundreds of examples where this
approach has succeeded in the role of indoctrination besides
resulting in rapid multiplication of the body.

While our society abounds today with examples of new
and creative approaches to the accomplishment of a great
variety of tasks, we as Christian believers must be alert to
new possibilities for the improvement of Christian education
in our churches.

Guiding Spiritual Development

A strong program of indoctrination must ultimately lead

to a point where members of the body live by these doctrinal persuasions with a sense of conviction. It is not enough to bring individual members to a level where they are able to merely parrot back doctrinal statements when asked for answers. An urgent imperative in this regard is expressed by Hollis L. Green:

> Churchmen must seek ways of getting the doctrine out of the book and into the hearts of the people. Doctrine is a firm foundation upon which to stand, but experience is necessary to storm the ramparts and reach to the uttermost parts of the earth with the transforming message of Christ.[5]

It is to be hoped that daily as members of the body move in their worlds, outsiders shall see lives which have been deeply affected by the church's efforts to indoctrinate. For this reason the church will have sought to bring the scriptural imperatives into a framework of Christian standards which are practical for our day. Though some will argue that the church has no right to set up rigid standards, the fact remains that the church is responsible to maintain the purity of its witness.

Setting up standards of Christian behavior need not be motivated by an improper desire to restrict and control, but rather because of a legitimate desire that Christian character be constantly demonstrated in the daily lives of believers. When we insist on adherence to Christian standards of behavior, we are assisting those within the body of believers to develop a life consistent with our Christian identification.

While we accept the fact that each individual is personally responsible for his own spiritual development, there is also a sense of corporate responsibility that cannot be avoided. In the building of a caring-sharing community of believers, the total body must be willing to assume its role in helping to guide each member to the maximum level of spiritual development.

7

Our Pastor Is a Caring-Sharing Person

Personal approach of the pastor

Results of numerous surveys reveal that a very small percentage of church attenders first began attending that church because of the particular pastor who serves that congregation. Most of the respondents indicated that they were first attracted to the church by the personal influence and invitation of family and friends.

In spite of the survey findings, I have never seen any responsible writing or report on church life which would depict the pastor as being unimportant to the success of the growing church. To the contrary, in my personal conversations with laypersons from many congregations which could be characterized as caring-sharing communities of believers, I have sensed that there is a deep respect for the pastor as one who they feel is one of the key agents in the success story.

Probably there are some pastors who have been at the right place at the right time and have fallen heir to a rich harvest which was actually due to such factors as strong lay leadership, a particularly unique ministry which caught fire, or a sudden impact of the area with new people. However, that man will not remain at the helm of that ship long unless he is able to rise to a level where he is able to exhibit strong leadership.

Thus we are interested in the kind of man who is vital to the building of a caring-sharing community of believers. Let us observe some of the elements of his personal approach which contribute to a fruitful ministry.

People Oriented

Some ministers have barely arrived at their charges when they begin to work on the steps toward the next move. It is not surprising that such career-oriented pastors are seldom recognized as the "doers."

Our church members are quick to recognize when a pastor is interested in serving people through Christ and ministering to their needs as a shepherd of the flock. His involvement in people's lives and sharing of lofty dreams for ministry serve to strengthen that conception.

One temptation which could ultimately lead the pastor away from the proper focus of his ministry is to become overly involved in and committed to social and community concerns which are so time demanding as to rob him of achievement in his primary task. Initially this appears justifiable as an extension of his ministry, but eventually it could lead to a selfish pursuit of recognition as one's career image flourishes by coming to know prestigious people and receiving abundant publicity. Leonard Griffith highlights this in his book *We Have This Ministry:*

> The greatest single problem that ministers face is the problem of priorities, not only in the allotment of time and energy to specific tasks but in the allotment of life itself. We need to soak our souls in the priorities of Jesus and be reminded constantly that persons come first. Our careers are made for persons, not persons for our careers.[1]

Whenever a pastor becomes enamored with his professional importance as a career minister, he has a tendency to hole up in his office and effectively isolate himself from his people. Eugene L. Stowe quotes Russell Dicks, "Pastoral work consists more of going to the people than it does in their coming to him, for the pastor who goes to his people ultimately will find them coming to him."[2]

Depth of Commitment

Desirable characteristics in a pastor by some people's standards may include skill in communication, cleverness in manipulation, proficiency for motivation, adeptness in management, brilliance in public relations, etc. However, the quality which most contributes to a pastor's acceptance as a spiritual leader is his spiritual commitment to the fulfillment of his calling as a workman in God's great vineyard. An expansion of this idea comes from Eugene Skelton, as quoted by Larry Lewis:

> The quality of leadership that seems to mean the most is not so much a dynamic personality as it is a depth of commitment. The people of the church respond to the depth of the pastor's desire to reach people for Bible study and Christ.[3]

In conversations with laypersons it becomes readily apparent that there is a willingness to overlook deficiencies in certain skills when they perceive that their pastor is committed to leading his church into areas of achievement to which the Holy Spirit is pointing. Though personal charisma on the part of the leader may be temporarily sought, believers within the body who take the longer view know that spiritual commitment is of far greater value.

Dedication to spiritual excellence should also include the willingness to forego any selfish considerations when functioning as God's workman. Where competencies are lacking,

others must be found to perform needed tasks. These personnel so selected must not only be given authority to do their
work but must be respected as fellow laborers in this great
venture to which God has called us. Our love for Christ and
His Church enables us to forget our natural inclination to
reach out to praise and honor.

Ultimately, the only recognition that really counts will be
the words of our Lord at the end of life's race, "Well done,
thou good and faithful servant." The pastor who is committed to spiritual excellence and thus content to wait for God's
seal of approval will be regarded as a trustworthy servant.

Willingness to Share

Some years ago an urgent message was relayed to us by
telephone while we were meeting in the midweek prayer and
praise service. One of our young members who had been
critically ill had just lost vital signs of life and was being
sustained by life support systems. We were being requested
to gather as a congregation at the altar and anoint a friend of
hers with oil as we prayed for her healing. This request was
honored and a tremendous sense of assurance marked our
assembly. Later we were to learn that signs of life returned
even as we prayed, and her healing did result.

Following the prayer at the altar, I shared with the group
an experience from prior years when our infant son was
critically ill. During that Sunday morning service an elderly
man in the church had asked to be anointed with oil in my
son's behalf as we prayed for his healing. From the moment
of that prayer at the altar our son began to improve. While
relating the story, I choked up with emotion and was somewhat embarrassed at my lack of control. After the service was
dismissed, one of our key laymen thanked me for sharing the
experience. I responded rather apologetically as I mentioned
my inability to control my emotions. I'll never forget his

reply: "Pastor, it's helpful for us to know that pastors are human too."

Unfortunately a great many pastors have been convinced that it would be harmful to their leadership image to reveal points of weakness. Exactly the opposite effect has been experienced. Laypersons found it difficult to accept and identify with someone who seemed to be superhuman and thus could know little about their problems, hurts, and limitations. Even worse, some strongly questioned his credibility.

Not only is it advantageous for the pastor to reveal his humanness, but there needs to be an openness which permits him to voice concerns about controversial issues. Speaking of renewal in the church, Richards states:

> A pastor exerts a moral force which opens up the possibilities of change when (1) he becomes a human being to his congregation, (2) he trusts his real self to them, sharing his problems, his feelings, his ideas, his convictions, his experience of God's love, and when (3) he learns to speak his convictions freely without attempting to persuade, and with no aura of superiority involved.[4]

There seems to be a desperate need for open, honest communication between pulpit and pew. The pastor who is willing to share helps to facilitate koinonia.

Loves His People

One Sunday morning just prior to the pronouncement of the benediction, I said, "I just feel this morning I'd like to tell you that I love you." It was just that simple.

Present in the service was a man with his family who had come to our church that day after having located our address in the yellow pages. His self-image was at an all-time low, and by his own testimony he felt that no one really loved him or cared. Later he was to tell me that those words literally sent chills through him. A need had been met.

70

Certainly there are many who need to hear a message that conveys love, but the vast majority will need more than mere words to be convinced. They'll be analyzing his conversation, scrutinizing his conduct, and most hazardous of all, speculating as to his true motive. Getz contends:

> His personality must say in no uncertain way, "I love you, I care about you, I am here beside you, you can talk to me anytime, anywhere and about anything you wish. I won't condemn you! I won't hurt you! I will help you become the person you really want to become—a mature member of the body of Christ."[5]

Much of the pastor's leadership potential is determined by his ability to communicate the fact that he really cares. From time to time he is challenging his people to make commitments, to demonstrate loyalty, and to accept possible sacrifices in order to contribute to the building of the caring-sharing community of believers. Few are willing to follow the pastor in assuming these obligations unless they are convinced that he really loves them.

J. Oswald Sanders calls our attention to a great leader in the Early Church:

> Paul's greatness and successful leadership lay in no small measure in his ability to capture and to hold the intense love and loyalty of the friends with whom he freely mixed. True, he involved his friends in all sorts of risks for Christ's sake and the gospel's, but they followed him cheerfully because they were assured of his love for them.[6]

In a time when many modern seminaries and training schools are playing down the necessity for pastoral calling, this may well be our strongest vehicle for communicating love. Pastors need to interact with their people by rejoicing with them in their successes, crying with them when they hurt, and expressing interest in the daily routine of their lives.

Any pastor who has lived with his people during the week is a more effective preacher in the pulpit on Sunday.

Lifts Up Christ

Though it is important that the members of the body sense that the pastor loves and cares for them, a more certain word is required. Pastors are vulnerable to failure. Those who have only come to recognize the love of this human leader have been cheated.

A leading exponent of the positive approach, Robert Schuller offers this exhortation to pastors:

> There is after all, one unfilled need that exists in every human heart every Sunday. Every Christian and every non-Christian comes to church needing a fresh encounter with the inspiring, encouraging, new-hope-producing Spirit of the Eternal God. Bring Christ alive into their minds and hearts and you'll be a winner in the pulpit.[7]

The pastor who really cares for his people will have a burning desire to share with them the great riches of God's grace which offers hope in the practical experiences of life. This desire will lead him to diligently prepare himself to offer the scriptural word of encouragement and instruction. Having interacted with the laity in their battlefield and bathed his heart in Bible study and prayer, he stands before them each week with a message from God which finds ready acceptance.

Laypersons tend to interpret this excellence of ministry as an indication that the pastor views his assignment conscientiously and therefore truly cares. What an opportunity awaits every pastor every Lord's Day as people gather to hear a word from God!

Inspires Confidence

Some time ago a young lady who had been experiencing

marital difficulty came to share the fact that she had sought legal counsel and was calling it "quits" so far as the marriage was concerned. In prior weeks I had counseled with both of the partners in the marriage, and naturally I was disappointed.

As she shared some of the intimate details of the deteriorating relationship, I began to see that there was little hope for rescuing the marriage. In an attempt to keep the door open for future counsel and hopefully still be able to offer redemptive help, I said, "I'm your friend. You do know that, don't you?" She immediately replied, "I wouldn't have told you all I have if I didn't believe that."

The confidence this counselee had in her pastor was not developed overnight. By that time there was a length of pastoral tenure of several years which had enabled her to establish trust.

Church growth textbooks tell us that a pastor's most productive years on the pastorate are the fifth, sixth, and seventh years. Unfortunately, the great majority of pastors fail to reach even that fifth year before moving on to the next assignment. It is small wonder that the confidence level between pastor and people remains low in so many situations. Time is required for the pastor to inspire confidence.

Not only is time an important element in inspiring confidence, but in the numerous pastoral encounters the spiritual leader of the congregation must be viewed as credible. His growing credibility makes it possible for him to offer counsel, speak plainly where it is required, rebuke upon certain occasions, and proclaim the Scriptures as they relate to the current issues of the day—all this without strong resistance because he is viewed as a man of God.

Peter Wagner states that "the pastor of a growing church is typically a strong authority figure and that authority has been earned through living relationships with the people."[8]

A pastor who truly cares for his people and their relationship to the body wants to develop a community of believers which has the capacity to function effectively without his close supervision. Girard observes that "a church overly dependent on its pastor always suffers statistical losses when the pastor moves to another church, or even when he merely goes on vacation."[9]

There are numerous situations in which the pastor could perform required tasks faster and better than the untrained laymen. However, to yield to this temptation severely limits the pastor's ministry and denies the laity the opportunity to become productive members of the body. The pastor's role is that of an equipper or facilitator. Though it may seem to be a slow and tedious route, there is a tremendous amount of personal satisfaction when formerly unskilled laborers begin to function as master workmen in God's great vineyard.

Not only is this training process important just in terms of being able to multiply ministry, but the layperson soon recognizes that this pastor cares when he is willing to share the work load. The increasing efficiency with which the layman performs his work brings a greater joy in participation and in turn complements the work of the pastor.

It has been said that the congregation tends to take on the personality of the pastor. This is a frightening prospect to the conscientious leader, but God's servants are not left alone in their endeavor. Leslie Parrott reminds us that "the Holy Spirit will help a man develop a style of leadership that brings out the best in people."[10]

8

I Feel Close to God and the Family

Sherry never missed a service at her church; and whenever she entered the doors, she did so with a smile and a cheerful greeting. Her life situation apart from church was anything but encouraging. Both of her parents were drunk the majority of the time. There were several children in the family, and none of them received proper nourishment. Constant verbal conflict and fighting characterized her home most of the time. Yet the faith Sherry had received through her association with the church held her steady amidst the most discouraging circumstances.

One Sunday morning someone who met her at the door asked her how it was that with her difficult situation in life she could be so cheerful when she came to church. She hastily responded, "When I come to church, I feel close to God and the family."

Admittedly, not everyone who enters our doors on Sundays lives with the same set of problems as did Sherry, but each one nevertheless has his own hurts and needs to experience a closeness to God and the church family. In seeking to

75

build a caring-sharing community of believers, there is a need to develop a style of worship which will enable those with varying kinds of hurts and needs to experience a closeness of fellowship to God and the family.

Advance Preparation

Exciting and worshipful services don't just happen. Rather they come about as a result of careful planning. Although we cannot program the unique ministry of the Holy Spirit, it is possible to so structure our services that awareness of His presence may be increased and receptivity to His ministry enhanced.

By advance preparation, I am not referring to the preparation of the order of service which is to be printed in the worship folder. This is certainly better than no preparation at all, but too often arranging the order of service becomes a routine matter and actually contributes very little in guiding the assembly toward a specific worship focus.

Proper preparation involves the determination of a central purpose around which the service will be structured. This enables the leaders themselves to have a more clear sense of direction regarding the service. As Anne Ortlund observes, "If the up-front people aim at nothing, they can be sure they'll hit it every time."[1]

Selection of a theme or purpose may revolve around a vast variety of needs, crucial questions, social issues, challenges, and doctrinal emphases. It is noteworthy that all worshipers may feel good about the service being directed to a specific need area which seems to bypass part of the worshipers. For example, a service which centers upon the needs of youth can be appreciated by all when koinonia is at work in the body. Each worshiper knows that when careful planning is occurring, his specific needs will be addressed on occasion. Furthermore his caring-sharing attitude makes it possible for him to feel good when others' needs are being met.

Recently our Sunday morning service centered around the proper response to the experience of bereavement. Certainly not all of my congregation was at that moment in a state of grief. In fact, some of them had never experienced bereavement occasioned by the death of someone close to them. Nevertheless, all who were present either had experienced or would at some future point experience loss by death and could thus profit by hearing what God had to say to them.

Once the purpose has been determined, attention needs to be given to every detail of the service. Each component of the service should make a contribution to the realization of the purpose. Care should be taken not to introduce anything which detracts from the central purpose. All who have input to the service and will be participating should correlate their efforts and work as a team toward accomplishing the stated goal.

Planned Prayer Support

Before the purpose of the service is determined and components of the service are put together, prayer for the Holy Spirit's direction should have been much in evidence. Whenever we feel that our cleverness is adequate, we have fallen victims to our own self-delusions. Only as the Spirit directs us and assists us do we experience sufficiency.

In addition to the prayerful planning of the leadership, there are others who could make a contribution in prayer support which would greatly strengthen the service. Though not everyone will be participants in the leadership role, no one needs to be excluded from the privilege of praying for the success of the assembly of the believers.

Numerous methods are available to lead the maximum

number of our people to pray earnestly for God's will to be realized in the worship service. Only those who have been a part of the prayer support system are in a favorable position to experience God's choice blessings and help in the worship gathering. Prayer cells may be organized and alerted to pray for the service. A certain area may be designated where volunteers may gather prior to the service to join in prayer. Some churches are bringing large groups together on Saturday night to pray for the Sunday services as well as other concerns. Even though some personal schedules may not adapt well to these special prayer cells, all should be encouraged to be active in prayer at certain given times that the will of God may be accomplished as the members of the body gather to worship.

Increased Involvement

Girard states that we "have depended too long on the ministry of one man. . . . God has given every believer in Christ a ministry to the other members of the Body. Until each of us begins to find his ministry, the church will never really be healthy."[2]

Though Girard's statement relates to a ministry which does not necessarily have to be confined to the public service, could it be that the failure to include more lay participants in the service itself has been a colossal mistake?

Traditionally, the main participants have been the pastor, other pastoral staff, choir members, musicians, and ushers. Other support personnel who serve at a greater distance and yet fill a vital need include children's church workers, nursery staff, sound engineers, etc. Yet there is that great untapped majority who faithfully occupy their pews each week.

One pastor has a different layperson each week share a 60-second stewardship testimony immediately prior to receiving the collection of tithes and offerings. You can readily see that this procedure not only increases the number of participants in the service but also potentially could increase the level of stewardship awareness.

In many churches a layperson reads a scripture lesson during the service. Over a period of time many people are given an opportunity to minister in this way.

Anne Ortlund describes a most interesting Sunday morning event in her husband's church which she calls the "Sunday morning huddle." Prior to the service those who are to participate in a major way gather in the pastor's office to discuss the purpose of the service and what special things are to happen and why. Specific instructions are given when necessary, and then the group prays together for the success of this spiritual endeavor. The entire group feels a sense of responsibility for the service and understands the direction they are headed. Since there is a different layperson reading the Scriptures each week, over a period of time a great number of the members of the body catch the feel of what happens, and as a result more people in the pews are responding in positive ways.

Music That Moves

Since a great part of my life has been wrapped up in music, I tend to regard music as one of the most important elements in the worship service. However, it appears I am not alone. The many references in the Book of Psalms lead me to believe that the Psalmist shared my feeling. Then I note Paul's statement, "Speaking to yourselves in psalms and hymns and spiritual songs, singing and making melody in your heart to the Lord" (Eph. 5:19).

Good music not only attracts others who enjoy listening, but it also enables the worshiper to express praise in a measure he might be unable to do under other circumstances.

Life's complexities have a way of inflicting moods upon

us which center our thoughts upon selfish interests. Spirited singing by the congregation or choir enables the worshiper to gain freedom from his tensions and ultimately experience the joy of releasing himself to the work of the Holy Spirit. In this spirit of abandon the singing becomes an expression of devotion and praise to God.

Not to be overlooked is the value of our ministry to each other through the medium of music. Worshiping with us in the pews are countless others who have suffered life's hurts during the week who are led into a spirit of praise by our participation in the worship experience of "singing and making melody in our hearts to the Lord."

Certainly not every church will be blessed with the same degree of musical talent. Very small churches may find it difficult to even maintain a choir. Yet in view of the great contribution music offers to the service, wise leadership must seek to use whatever resources are available to the greatest advantage. Sometimes even a small church develops a reputation for its enthusiastic music because the people are led to sing heartily the great songs of praise. Behold! it is not long a small church.

Informality Leads to Sharing

The various worship forms we follow which are designed to gather our people in true worship serve a worthwhile purpose and should not be lightly cast aside in favor of a haphazard approach to worship. Yet there does seem to be a need to seek ways of eliminating the stiffness of manner and arrangement which often characterize the service and hinder the desired freedom of response.

Over a period of years I have observed that where I have been, the service has begun with the entry of the choir and the pastor's call to worship from the podium. Since the action takes place up front, there seems to exist a psychological chasm between the worshipers in the pews and the participation at the front.

In my attempt to bridge this apparent gap, I have employed the prelude period as an opportunity to greet some of the worshipers in their pews. At a certain point a soloist or ensemble presents a special musical rendition designed to heighten expectancy for the approaching service. At the conclusion of this musical number, I take a microphone in hand in the area of the front rows of pews and extend a greeting to the congregation by saying, "Good morning." This elicits a response. Then I continue in a relaxed manner to share some special blessings God has given to our church during the week, occasionally highlight some special event that is forthcoming, and perhaps mention my excitement about the theme of the service and what God is going to do in our lives during the hour of worship. The people are then asked to stand and welcome the other worshipers to our church. During this time of friendship expression, barriers tend to disappear and even visitors are caused to feel more comfortable in a strange environment. Our people now freely move across the aisle or to other rows of pews to be sure visitors are greeted. While the congregation is still standing, I begin a chorus which brings us into an attitude of worship. Before the chorus is completed, I go to the platform as the music director takes over and completes the transition.

This procedure has been helpful to me and has worked in my situation. You may discover a better approach for your church which leads your people to participate more fully in a caring-sharing ministry. I hope you will not be afraid to be creative. The variety you introduce may be refreshing.

Variety Adds Spice

There's a restaurant located in proximity to our church. Quite often I go there for lunch on weekdays because its location is so convenient and the food is tasty. However, one drawback which forces me to go elsewhere on occasion is the very limited menu. Frankly, I enjoy variety, and at that point this restaurant fails to satisfy my desires.

I suspect that a great many worshipers may feel this way on occasion when the routine of the services has become so predictable that a printed order of worship is unnecessary. Even in our worship services, it can be refreshing to experience variety in form, order, and content.

Some months ago I changed the order of worship in our morning service which was centered around our quarterly observance of Holy Communion. Instead of the usual meditation just prior to receiving the elements of the Lord's Supper, I presented the Communion message in three parts separated by intervals of time when music and other acts of worship directed our attention to the changes God desired to effect in our lives. Also the bread and the cup were served at different points in the service so as to maximize our appreciation for God's provision of salvation through Jesus Christ, His Son.

The Communion service turned out to be a very precious time when God's presence was so warmly felt by those attending. Expressions of appreciation for that particular service were numerous. Although I would not discount the movement of the Holy Spirit among us that day, I really believe that changing the order of worship contributed to a freshness of approach which caused the worshipers to be more open to the ministry of the Spirit.

Over an extended period of time, coming up with fresh innovations and new approaches can be time consuming, but the benefits seem to justify the special effort required.

Attitude of Expectancy

What happens in the worship services over an extended

period of time reveals to the congregation the extent of planning that has gone into each service occasion. When the members of the body begin to sense that extensive preparation is being given to each service and the results are evident, there is an attitude of expectancy that builds up in the minds of the members.

Parrott suggests that we should seek to "make every Sunday an event."[3] To accomplish this objective, we can allow no slackness in service planning. Every Sunday is viewed as a fresh opportunity to minister to the unique needs of the people who attend. We dare not disappoint them on any Lord's Day, for that may be the occasion of their greatest need.

In Wagner's optimistic approach to church growth, he states that "when a lot of people come together, hungry to meet God, a special kind of worship experience can occur. That experience is what I call 'celebration.'"[4]

Our awareness that people are coming to the weekly celebration expecting to receive something which will satisfy their hunger should serve to impress upon us a strong desire to make each Lord's Day eventful. Everyone in leadership roles must respond to this challenge—pastors, music directors, musicians, and directors of youth and children's ministries.

One course of action which I have followed in an effort to strengthen the attitude of expectancy is to pursue series preaching or preaching through a Bible book. When this is done with emphasis on bringing the truths to bear upon the practical concerns of life, the people receive blessing and look with expectancy to the next time of assembly.

To God Be the Glory

In all our efforts to create a worship style which allows for a closeness of fellowship with God and the family, we cannot be satisfied until we sense that our people are responding in positive ways to the building of a caring-sharing community of believers. Upon the realization that this is truly happening, there may well be a temptation to pride ourselves in our accomplishments. Succumbing to such a temptation serves to negate the apparent achievements. It must be remembered that only God can create koinonia, and we are only the the instruments of His working.

Anne Ortlund quotes Dr. A. W. Tozer as he illustrates a wrong interpretation of people's responses:

> It's the first Palm Sunday, and here comes Jesus riding into Jerusalem on a donkey. The crowds begin to shout "Hosanna!" The old donkey pricks up his ears. Some in the crowd throw their coats in the road; others spread out palm branches.
>
> "Well!" says the donkey, switching a fly off a mange patch. "I had no idea they really appreciated me like this! Listen to those hosannas, would you. I must really be something."[5]

In her reaction to Tozer's account, Ortlund declares, "Friends, if anybody comes around after the service, saying, 'Wow! That was terrific!'—they're not actually saying hosanna to you. All you did was bring Jesus to them."[6]

If we succeed to any degree in developing a worship style which contributes to the building of a caring-sharing community of believers, it is because God has helped us. To God be the glory!

9

Do My Ideas Count?

The occasion was a family Christmas gathering, and as a young teen I was seated with my uncles while one of the issues of the day was being discussed. Feeling very strongly on one particular point of the discussion, I interjected my viewpoint. Suddenly I observed that everyone was turned toward me, and they were intently taking in what I was saying. Then further conversation evolved as a result of what I had said.

That was a high moment in my young life, for finally a group that I respected was accepting what I had to say, and I felt that my ideas really counted for something. Of course, the difference in attitude of acceptance had come about because of my attainment of an age which spoke of some degree of maturity.

Within the church, age may not be the key factor in gaining acceptance for our viewpoints. Rather, leadership tends to be more readily influenced by length of tenure with the organization, prior demonstration of acceptance by the total body, prestigious occupation, social status, and enviable financial position.

Is it any wonder that the "average person" who seems to

fit into none of the acceptance categories asks the question, "Do my ideas count?"

Everyone Makes a Contribution

In nearly 2,000 years of church history, if there is any lesson that we should have learned well, it is that each member of the body makes a contribution. Though some may seem to make a greater impact than do others, we dare not discount the worth of any one person.

Paul warns us against assigning the seemingly less capable and less prestigious to a position of lesser importance. Instead he writes to us under divine inspiration, "Those members of the body, which seem to be more feeble, are necessary; and those members of the body, which we think to be less honourable, upon these we bestow more abundant honour" (1 Cor. 12:22-23).

Your church cannot become the caring-sharing community of believers God intended it should be unless provision is made for every member of the body to have a part. Furthermore, there must be a willingness to accept the contribution of the individual members.

In our society we have become overly concerned on occasion with the concept of perfection. This is unfortunate because most of what we do falls far short of this concept. Therefore, we tend to feel unfulfilled and depressed when our contributions appear to fall into the nonperfect category.

A further problem in this regard comes when we reject the contributions of others because they fail to measure up to the ideal. Although that rejection may not be direct, it is thus interpreted when we respond with a lack of enthusiasm and no expression of appreciation.

Those in the body who desire to offer ideas for improvement of ministry are soon silenced by a leadership structure which allows no means for input. When it is sensed that the ideas of any one individual do not really count, there is less involvement and eventually less commitment.

Each of us is strengthened when others within the body minister to us and us to them. Because we are all members of the same body, our individual contributions are essential for proper function. We must create an atmosphere where everyone feels his contribution really counts.

Ownership of Goals

Few of us would question the importance of setting optimistic, faith-inspiring goals for the purpose of advancing the cause of Christ through our own organization. Though there is considerable difference in the quality of goals, there are probably few churches which have not at certain times set goals for accomplishment.

The major problem then is not so much concerned with the existence of goals as it is with who has determined the goals. It is a rather common occurrence that goals are formulated by a rather limited and elite leadership group. Not only is the majority of the body denied input, but often their needs and desires are given little or no consideration. This course of action confirms the previously held suspicion that their ideas do not count.

In his book dealing with cooperation between pastor and laity in the tasks of ministry, James L. Garlow defines a "good goal" as "one in which the persons responsible for implementing it and living with the consequences of it were involved in formulating it."[1]

All of us feel much more comfortable with goals we have helped to form. When we are given the opportunity to participate in the creation of goals, there is a far greater readiness to make commitments to seeing the goals through to completion. "We are much more likely to want to work on something that has been our own idea."[2]

One argument offered for setting goals at higher levels is that the majority of the body has no desire or willingness to share in this task. Yet those who seek to bring members from all levels into the process discover the opposite to be true. Not only is there desire to contribute and willingness to cooperate, but ideas of outstanding quality often come from the least expected sources.

Another argument proposed is that time is lost when too many are given opportunity to introduce their ideas. Probably we will have to admit that the time element in goal setting will be lengthened by the inclusion of all. However, the real compensation is realized when all of those involved in formulating the goals, accept them, commit themselves to them, and begin working toward their attainment. No time will need to be spent in attempting to determine why the goals were not accepted and eventually achieved.

Dreaming Together

Never shall I forget a certain layman in a church I served who was a great "idea man." He was too impatient and too concerned with perfection to follow through on the implementation of these ideas. Nevertheless, there was no limit to his ability to dream great dreams. Consequently, I remember that I used to get with him often so we could dream together.

In that same church there were people who lacked the ability to dream as did their brother, but they enjoyed working with great ideas, finding ways to bring them into reality, and pursuing them with all diligence. Sometimes a side benefit was realized when the workers came up with creative ideas while putting the original dream into a plan of action. Thus the dream was expanded.

On the first Sunday of January one year, I handed out a "Dream Sheet" to each worshiper present. The idea for this had come from Dayton and Engstrom's description of a procedure they had used at World Vision International. Only two questions were included on the sheet: "What are your dreams for our church this year? What are your dreams for what God might do with and through us 10 years from now?"[3]

That Sunday morning I encouraged my people to fill out their "Dream Sheets" at their leisure and return them within two weeks to a box for that purpose in the foyer. Not all the sheets were returned, but a sizeable number were, and the dreams shared were very encouraging and challenging. Over the next several days I wrote a personal note to each of the respondents, thanking them for sharing their dreams with me, and asking them to join me in prayer that these dreams might become reality within the context of God's will. My personal note really was saying to them that their ideas do count.

One church has devised a method for constant input of ideas described by Schaller and Tidwell. In the pew racks are cards with the simple words "I wish" at the top. Any response which fits with the two-word opener is possible. Naturally there are occasional gripes which could be viewed as negative ideas but also could be considered as positive suggestions for change or correction. Of obvious benefit are the frequent creative ideas which people feel free to offer. The members of that organization must feel that their ideas are considered worthwhile.[4]

Taking Proper Advantage

Whether ideas of individual members are secured by surveys, personal conferences, brainstorming sessions, etc., we will eventually come to know a great deal about the persons who contribute the ideas if we take the time for analysis. Wise is the leader who is interested in the person as well as the idea.

The flow of ideas from certain persons may reveal potential for a deeper level of leadership. Much can be learned about the person and the way he thinks by his expression of ideas. As specific abilities are revealed or a sense of dedication becomes evident, you will want to take proper advantage of these qualities by moving to involve the individuals in a shared-leadership role.

Building a caring-sharing community of believers requires the active involvement of the total body. Thus we must be alert to the emergence of those persons to whom God has evidently granted a gift for leadership. It is a fact that many of these persons are so marked by the spirit of humility that they will not thrust themselves into the forefront. They will wait for us to take proper advantage of the situation and assign them to a job.

There are yet others who possess the leadership characteristics required but will need to be motivated before they can be expected to make any major contribution. Our taking proper advantage in such cases may mean a costly investment in time and interest in order to bring these persons to be the persons God intended them to be.

Learning to Trust

Frequently the potential contributions that individual members can make are lost, not because the leadership structure is disinterested but because there is a fear of trusting. Included in this hesitancy may be a fear of increased responsibility and introduction to a new set of risks. Both of these are very real possibilities but should not deter the committed leader.

Parrott describes the "plus-plus pastor or layman" as the kind of leader who not only "has great confidence in his own skills but has an equal confidence in the skills and abilities of others."[5]

The critical need of our learning to trust others who

stand ready to make a contribution to the building of a caring-sharing community of believers is beautifully illustrated in this story as related by Jenkins:

> One day a stranger passed down the streets of a city in Europe and entered the door of a cathedral. An organist and hungry for music, he sought opportunity to play the organ. He found the old man who was the church's organist, explained his desire to play, and asked if he might have permission to play the organ. At first the older man refused, fearing that the younger man had some scheme to oust him from his position. But the stranger assured him that he had no ulterior motive, that he had heard what a great organ it was and only wanted to try it out. Finally the old man reluctantly consented but watched with an air of suspicion as if he feared the stranger might carry his organ away.
>
> The young man sat down at the organ and ran his fingers over the keys—floods of tender, mellow, wonderful music poured forth. The stranger pulled out another set of stops and greater tones poured forth sweeter than before. Another set of stops and still another set of stops with colorings of melody and rhapsodies of music the old man did not dream were in his organ! When the great instrument came on in full power, the whole cathedral trembled with the sweeping resonance of the mighty music; and when the stranger came to the climax, the finale, the old organist stood there with tears streaming down his face.
>
> He walked over to the stranger and said, "Stranger, tell me who you are, Sir. What is your name?" The stranger modestly answered, "My name is Mendelssohn." The old man placed his hand on the young man's shoulder, and through his tears said, "Mendelssohn, Mendelssohn, the master, and how nearly I came to shutting you out! I would never have known what beautiful music was in my organ had you not played."[6]

10

What's Going On?

Communication procedures

My television viewing time is constantly interrupted by a series of commercial messages which are intended to convince me of the desirability of a product or service. Although I have not requested this information, never do I observe even the slightest hesitancy in sending it my way.

These merchandisers seem to be anxious to let me know about any technological breakthrough which has made it possible for them to offer me a better or new product. In the event a special opportunity is offered to more easily acquire their product or receive their service, they go to great lengths to make me aware of it and keep me informed about the amount of time I have to take advantage of the unique opportunity.

By contrast with the business community, the church has tended to do so little advertising that one would think there was an attempt to keep it all a secret. This is not only true as to our sharing of information with the general public but even as it relates to internal communication.

Our story promises to be more exciting and offers greater benefits than the messages of the commercial industry. It ought to be shared. Because of its possibilities, superb means of communication should be employed. We need to tell our story so well and advertise so extensively that no one needs to ask, "What's going on?" Let's tell them!

Promotion

The most common utilization of communication procedures is designed to promote what is going to be happening in the church. Hopefully, it is done so well that there is greater awareness and heightened interest, thus assuring increased involvement.

There is no need to be apologetic about doing extensive promotion. Some people may object on occasion because they feel that promotion is overdone, but the fact remains that without heavy promotion our church program will suffer from lack of participation. Again we do ourselves a favor by observing the advertising methods of our commercial counterparts.

Awareness of what is going on and what we are planning to do in the future is essential if we expect cooperation for any specific event. Though a need exists to advertise appealing events in such a manner as to attract those outside the active constituency, we dare not neglect internal communication needs. Schaller speaks of the quality of internal communication:

> People do respond to that which they are aware of and do not respond to that which they are not aware of in the life of the church. Thus, the deterioration of the quality of the internal communication often is wrongly diagnosed as a lack of responsiveness or a decline in interest among the members rather than as a decline in the quality of internal communication.[1]

Of course, we will be concerned with keeping people informed as to times and places of public meetings and events throughout the week. In addition to the normal schedule of activities, there needs to be an effort made to acquaint everyone with the various fellowship opportunities offered either by age or interest grouping. A list of special service possibilities and announcements of the available Bible study groups and how to become a part represent a needful area of our communication responsibility.

Promotion within the church is pursued in a great many ways, but the ordinary approach is to make full use of Sunday bulletins, weekly newsletters, telephone brigades, direct mail, and public announcements. Probably this list of common procedures should not be considered as a pick-and-choose situation, but rather a situation where all of the possibilities will need to be tapped.

To get our promotional message to those outside the body will necessitate other approaches and greater expense. Newspaper ads and possibly even radio and TV spots are desirable means of getting the promotional message to a broader base. With the increasing popularity of cable TV systems, television advertising may offer greater promise for the future because of the small cost factor. We should not hesitate to move as quickly as possible into these new media opportunities.

Celebrating Accomplishments and Victories

Too often in the church significant accomplishments and victories go unnoticed by the great majority of the body. Those persons who are closer to the source of action are aware of these special occasions for rejoicing and may even share their excitement by word of mouth with a selected few. However, it needs to be recognized that sharing these triumphs with the total constituency offers one of the greatest possibilities for celebration.

Within the context of public services and small-group meetings, there has been no hesitation to share needs for which prayer support is desired. Probably the most of these shared needs are met with positive responses as we have prayed. Yet so often the fact of victory and answered prayer is never reported, and the body loses the special opportunity to celebrate.

In most of our churches the most active arm of the organization is the Sunday School. Where creativity exists and alert Christian education personnel are applying the finest techniques to the education task, there are bound to be some exciting things happening. Yet a perusal of the average church newsletter reveals only a matter of statistics when reporting on the Sunday School. If something good is happening and it probably is, then let's tell about it. The body has a right to know.

Building a caring-sharing community of believers would suggest that we are not only concerned with the accomplishments of the organization, but of special concern and interest will be the celebrations and victories of individual members. Reporting these successes through communication channels affords everyone in the body an opportunity to celebrate. Paul's special treatment of the proper functioning of the Body of Christ as he wrote to the Corinthians reminds us that if "one member be honoured, all the members rejoice with it" (1 Cor. 12:26). If the body is to thus rejoice, we must let them know what's going on.

Sharing Dreams and Goals

The previous chapter dealt with the need to involve individuals in the task of planning and goal setting. Once the dreams have been shared and goals established at the leadership level, there is a need to communicate the finished product with the total congregation.

A significant number of the members will not become deeply involved in the planning and goal-setting process for a number of reasons. For example, there are those whose employment or unusual family problems limit the amount of time that may be shared. Their ability to attend the worship assemblies is possible only because of special planning and perhaps even some difficult concessions. Nevertheless, they will not have to be denied the privilege of knowing the direction that the Holy Spirit is taking this body of believers if dreams and goals are adequately communicated.

None of us who watched the television screens during the final days of the life of Martin Luther King, Jr., can ever forget those now famous words, "I have a dream!" In his moving speech televised to a nation of people who were aware that injustices existed, he articulated what the fulfillment of that dream would bring, and somehow as a nation we believed that it would come to pass even though great barriers were present.

While we agree that there is a great value in dreaming together in an effort to set goals which are faith-inspiring, we must also come to the conclusion that much is lost if we fail to communicate these dreams to the total body. The kind of conviction that King conveyed in the sharing of his dream must also characterize our sharing, whether it be by vocal presentation or the printed page.

Value of Recognition

Our volunteer service which contributes to the success of building a caring-sharing community of believers ought to be motivated by a love for Christ and His Church. However, we are human enough that we do respond positively to expressions of gratitude when that service has been rendered.

Every week in each of our churches there are people who make significant contributions of time, talent, and energy. Through the various communication tools available to us, we are able to give recognition to these dedicated servants. Schaller comments on the value of such recognition:

The congregation that systematically, intentionally, and publicly expresses its gratitude to the members, by name, for what they do in the life of that fellowship will make it easier for the old-timers and the newcomers to become better acquainted and to appreciate each other more as the weeks and months pass.[2]

A simple recognition of birthdays and anniversaries through our office communication can become a helpful tool in the building of a caring-sharing relationship. From church and Sunday School records, a file can be easily assembled which provides a ready list of all those who are observing such occasions for a particular week or month. Some churches list these in their newsletter weekly, whereas others do it each month.

One of my elderly members is confined in a home for the aged and only rarely is able to attend any of our services. However, using the published list of birthdays and anniversaries in the church's newsletter, she sends greeting cards along with a handwritten note. No longer able to maintain the level of activity she used to enjoy, this is her special ministry. Many of the newcomers know her only because of the cards she has sent.

If your church is fortunate enough to have equipment which allows you to print photographs, you would profit by always having a camera ready for instant use. Pictures provide some of the most useful ways of recognizing a person's involvement. A suggestion you might consider is including a picture of one of your families in each week's newsletter along with a biographical sketch. This procedure provides an excellent way to get acquainted with others of the body.

Projecting an Image

There is only one thing worse than failure to communicate—communicating poorly. I have observed some church bulletins and newsletters which were of such poor quality that great disservice to the church was done by their production.

Our printed materials represent a very modest investment in terms of financial cost but because of their wide exposure require our best efforts in preparation. We have no way of knowing how many people will be exposed to our church through this means. Therefore the material should be attractive, readable, and positive in tone.

In his handbook, Stoody reminds us that "since your parish paper represents your church and you believe that there is no more important or nobler institution, you will not be content with anything less than the best possible product."[3]

Perhaps a similar word needs to be expressed in regard to our churches using radio and television time for ministry exposure. There are few churches who possess the resources and personnel which are required to produce a radio or television program of quality. Anything less than a quality production is unjustified.

Much of what comes over the airways in the name of Christian ministry is a disgrace to the sponsoring organization and a reproach upon the Church at large. If a church sincerely desires to minister through this medium but lacks the resources and personnel to do quality production independently, they should seek out professional organizations who specialize in arranging production with the individual church as the sponsor.

Budget Conscious

In view of the pressures most of us face in these inflationary times, it has forced the church to be budget conscious. Ministries and services need to be evaluated to determine if we are keeping priorities in line and spending church funds wisely.

A great deal of money can be spent for church communications, or we can elect to limit expenditures to the minimum necessary to communicate effectively and yet maintain a quality standard which reflects the proper image.

Perhaps we would do ourselves a service by evaluating the returns gained from good communication procedures as compared to certain other ministries in the church. Most likely we will discover that even the purchase of good equipment and its maintenance represent a small expenditure as contrasted with other things we do and their relative cost factor.

The smallest church can afford a typewriter and mimeograph machine. In some cases small churches in the same geographic area may profit by sharing the same equipment and thus be able to purchase equipment capable of greater variety.

Churches of medium size and up can well justify adding to their mimeograph machine an electronic stencil cutter which makes it possible to produce printed materials with artwork and photographs. Even greater quality could be achieved by going to an offset press operation. Amazingly, the cost of this equipment could be less than many medium-sized churches spend for a bus which benefits only a few.

W. Curry Mavis sums it up well when he contends that "every local church can have effective publicity irrespective of the size of its advertising budget. . . . It is achieved in large part by having a well organized plan of publicity based on congregational enthusiasm for the work of the church."[4]

11

Building Bridges

Cultural differences

Over a period of many weeks I had ministered to a family in a way I had never ministered before. My ministry to them had involved many visits to the alcoholic unit of one of the community's hospitals as well as follow-up visits to their home and phone calls at odd hours when the struggles required an understanding listener. Both the mother and father were slaves to alcoholism, and their two small children had become unwilling victims.

Finally, the day arrived when they entered our sanctuary for the first time. Not accustomed to church attendance, they were not attired as were other worshipers around them. Yet their obvious hunger was evident as they tried to participate as fully as they knew how. Hanging on to every word I spoke, they responded with an unconcealed eagerness when at the end of the sermon I invited all who wanted to experience the joy of forgiveness to come forward to the public altar.

I really do believe our people sincerely tried to reach out to that family. Several caring Christians knelt with them at the altar that Sunday morning and counseled them as they gave their hearts to Christ. In succeeding weeks concentrated efforts were made to demonstrate love and understanding to a family of four who represented a different cultural background than most of us had experienced.

A tremendous sense of disappointment gripped me when one day as I visited in their home, they said, "Pastor, we just don't fit at that church with those people." Although the members of the body had tried to express love in a caring-sharing ministry, the cultural difference had been too great. We had failed to build a bridge that was adequate to span the gap.

The cultural differences which we confront may take many forms—social, racial, economic, language, etc. It really matters little what the nature of that difference is, for if there is a difference of any kind, we are faced with a problem which requires a solution, or our ministry is seriously curtailed.

The Problem of Homogeneity

An immediately discouraging message greets us when we begin to consider building bridges. All the church growth studies reveal that there is a homogeneous principle which has to be reflected upon whenever we begin to consider a ministry to different cultural groups within the same church.

Speaking as a representative of church growth experts, Wagner states that "a decade and a half of research dealing with numerous cultures in virtually every corner of the world confirms that the churches most likely to grow are those which bring together in the local fellowship those of a single homogeneous unit."[1]

Now we must recognize that this homogeneous principle is stated in regard to a local congregation. When we look at the church as a whole, an entirely different picture emerges. Stedman makes this observation:

> There is no group in the world so gloriously heterogeneous as the church. Its genius is that it is made up of

different kinds of people . . . The church crosses all the boundaries which men erect and all natural distinctions as well, and gathers all people, without exception, into one body.

But we do not ignore these boundaries easily. Friction often arises because of them.[2]

It is this last point which Stedman raises that is the source of our concern. Whenever friction is present in the local body of believers, growth is hindered. Yet this element of friction seems to plague us as these cultural differences develop into boundaries of great proportion.

Quite often a church comes into being composed by people of a single homogeneous unit. Because of the similarities which exist among them as to social and economic status in life, a beautiful harmony exists in the beginning days. This harmony of relationship enables them to join together in a unity of purpose as they seek to build a caring-sharing community of believers.

Problems nevertheless tend to enter the picture when the dynamics of individual life structures operate with varying degrees of movement. Promotions in the secular vocational role as well as changes in financial position serve to create a gap between the achievers and the nonachievers. Though the people are the same and their interest in serving Christ has not been affected, their interests are perceptibly different and even sets of values undergo changes.

Since human nature is such that people are disposed to view differences with suspicion, every word and every action becomes the source of possible friction. Unless bridges are built across these gaps, the increasing level of friction will ultimately destroy the unity of purpose originally experienced by the body, and growth will be retarded.

Even further problems are produced when large numbers of the body move into a stratum of society which is no longer representative of the community to which the church seeks to minister. In such cases those within the community who do respond positively may eventually feel the gap is too great and drift away. The net result is often a drying up of the church's ministry potential.

Differences Real or Felt

As a lad growing up in an environment lacking in economic advantage and knowing little of social prestige, I was a part of a small church whose members were mostly from a different stratum of life. However, I cannot recall that the real differences which were most certainly present were a problem to me. The members of that local fellowship of believers treated me as if no differences existed. Never do I remember a time when I felt I did not fit, although I definitely could see the wide variance in many of life's privileges.

This important distinction between real and felt differences and the impending consequences are addressed by Massey:

> Fellowship is not hindered by differences that are seen or known but by those that are felt. It is essential to both church worship and witness that every sharer be trained to regard himself and all the others as members. . . . When the point is truly understood, all attitudes, emotions, and equipment of temperament can be directed to the purposes of fellowship.[3]

Our unique opportunity lies in the development of a course of action which avoids any demonstration of non-acceptance either by revealed attitude or observable conduct. On the distinctly positive side, we can prove that we care by expressing love and support openly.

Referring to my own situation in the church of my roots, the efforts which were made to bridge the gap included invitations to various homes for meals and other fellowship occasions, gifts of a material nature which met a particular need of the moment, opportunities to minister through the use of God-given talents, appointment to leadership roles, and words of encouragement designed to give me a sense of self-worth. Because that community of believers reached out to me in a caring-sharing way, the real differences which definitely existed were not felt by me in any great measure.

Crossing Over to Them

When we come to believe that our Christian heritage obligates us to cross over barriers to minister to one another, we cannot ignore this persuasion without incurring guilt. Therefore, we are inclined to seek the best methods available that we may successfully cross over.

Just as we are about to begin, Wagner confronts us with this seemingly paradoxical statement:

> If the option of crossing homogeneous unit lines and mixing two or more different groups in the congregation is chosen, the positive effect is that Christians will feel very good about their success in breaking racial or class barriers. . . . However, . . . the evangelistic potential of the church will be seriously curtailed.[4]

Even though the foregoing statement presents an accurate picture of research studies in the matter of church growth, we must be guided by the Holy Spirit in our response to the Great Commission. My confidence in an omnipotent God leads me to believe that the concern of future evangelistic potential can well be left in God's hands. That is not our problem.

McGavran has been quoted as saying that "men like to become Christians without crossing racial, linguistic or class barriers."[5] Acceptance of this fact forces us to conclude that we must not only build the bridges but also cross over to them and minister on their turf.

In seeking to cross over, it is necessary for us to identify the gap by learning all we can about the person or persons to whom it is our desire to minister. The time spent in identification of the cultural pattern may be lengthy and thus produce a state of impatience, but we may be assured it is time well spent. Until we understand the differences, we cannot know how great is the distance we will be required to cross.

When we have successfully reached a group of people from another culture, the opportunity then exists for sending a team of converts to evangelize among their own kind. Because they identify with the culture and therefore are able to communicate effectively, greater success is assured.

Paul Orjala calls our attention to two considerations which are valid to our efforts in crossing cultural gaps. "We may have to learn how to talk to them in a dialect other than the language of Zion."[6] Though on the surface we may appear to speak the same language, little do we realize how deeply ingrained our language has become with words, phrases, and clichés which are meaningless to those outside our own fold.

A second point addressed by Orjala is the simple element of sincerity. Our sincerity in presenting Christ, coupled with our dependence on the empowerment of the Holy Spirit, will make possible our crossing over the gap and bringing some into the family of God. The sincerity which characterizes our witness is recognized as an expression of love and thus Christ is properly represented.[7]

Not One, but Several

Failure in our attempt to bring those of other cultural groups into our community of believers is highly probable unless we are able to reach several within their particular culture. According to McGavran, this must be done "fairly rapidly." The goodness and helpfulness of the body is important but not adequate "to make them feel thoroughly at home. What they need is 15, 20, 50, or 100 people of that segment of society added. Then the church becomes their church."[8]

The concept which we are identifying here as "not one, but several" is offered only as a means for effectively bringing those representing cultural differences into the fellowship and providing for multiplication. Certainly there is no suggestion that the "one" is unimportant. It is to this point that Hollis Green speaks:

> The church must somehow see the overall culture and not lose sight of the individual and his personal needs . . . it is individuals that the church must reach. However, when a significant number of key individuals are reached, a whole group of people can often be truly influenced by the Christian message.[9]

In our earlier consideration of small-group dynamics, we may have touched on one of the most essential points of our role in bringing those won from other cultural segments of society to a place where they feel comfortable among us. The small group stands out as an effective vehicle for creating a ministry to each other as well as to others.

Interaction

The word *interaction* is one which Richards uses to describe a basic necessity to effect bridge-building:

> People do not develop a sense of community apart from frequent, regular social interaction with one another. . . . They have to share, to dig deep into their own lives with God and openly seek together His answers to their problems and needs.[10]

Involvement in each other's lives must be strongly desired and totally voluntary if interaction is to be productive. All interaction needs to seek its base in a firm commitment to the Word and to a goal, that the practical implications of the Word be identified in the lives of community members.

I believe that social interaction is essential on a continuous basis in the local body if we are to prevent gaps of a cultural nature from developing or widening. The task of building bridges never ceases if we seek to maintain harmony in the building of a caring-sharing community of believers.

The dynamic growth of individuals within the body requires that we exert great effort toward acquiring an understanding of one another so that we may minister to the whole man.

12

Building for Community

Church architecture

Our church board was gathered to consider agenda items which related to the building of our new church on a recently purchased 12-acre site. One of the men who had been an active churchman for many years related the fact that this was his first experience in planning for a totally new church.

My lay friend was not alone, for as I neared the quarter-century mark of pastoral service, this also represented my first encounter in this type of planning. There had been building projects which represented provision for additional space, but never had there been an opportunity to help plan a completely new church where some of the ideas I'd gathered across the years could possibly be incorporated.

This was a tremendously exciting adventure as we gave consideration to the ways in which our new building could enable us to more effectively pursue our mission as a church. We naturally envisioned that this new facility would expand and improve our opportunities.

However, we tried to keep in mind that simply building a new structure and thereby releasing ourselves from the restrictions that the old property imposed would not of itself solve every problem. The fact that many church organizations have approached this task with erroneous thinking is indicated by Benjamin:

> Congregations sometimes make a sad mistake. They may think that a more adequate house of worship can serve as a substitute for individual concern. Legion are the congregations which have felt that a new church building would inspire a great increase in attendance. No house of worship, no matter how attractive, can take the place of love and fellowship.[1]

Theology of Church Buildings

Whenever conversation centers around the planning of church buildings, a whole range of questions comes forth. Are buildings really necessary? Can't we worship God just as effectively in homes or in community centers? Does the building have to be elaborate for us to fulfill our mission? Is God pleased with our stewardship when we spend all this money on a building which has such limited use?

All of the foregoing questions are legitimate. Not everyone agrees on the answers. Snyder comments that "theologically, church buildings are at best unnecessary and at worst idolatrous."[2] Yet I believe there is a theology of church buildings which is satisfactory for our age.

Old Testament worshipers according to earliest records available to us gathered in the open air before crude altars made of stones. When Moses led the nation of Israel out of Egypt, God instructed His people to build a Tabernacle which would become a portable building for worship and sacrifice. Then with the wilderness wanderings finally over, Solomon became God's agent to effect the construction of the Temple which in accord with God's instructions was of very elaborate design. The symbolism incorporated within the design of the Temple enabled sinful man to worship a holy God as man looked forward to a full revelation in Christ. Also during this period of man's history synagogues were erected to accommodate a teaching and preaching ministry.

In fulfillment of the promise, Christ came and went to Calvary. Christ's death at Calvary ended all need for Temple sacrifice and other Temple services.

One more significant event took place in the Upper Room on the Day of Pentecost when the Holy Spirit came and filled the hearts of the believers. No longer was God's presence limited to a place or a building, but rather He was now living in the lives of His people. As the Body of Christ, the Church, these believers began meeting in homes, in the open air, or wherever people gathered. Buildings were of little importance during the first few hundred years.

During the period just prior to the Dark Ages, great attention was given to cathedral construction. Buildings were deemed very important, but spirituality had declined to a low level. The past few hundred years have seen a variety of approaches to church building.

From *Church Building Sourcebook 2* comes this view concerning the purpose of the church building:

> The church building should not become an end in itself for a New Testament congregation. The building should be a symbol to the community at large. However, the building is more than a symbol; it is the place where the community of faith comes together. This coming together is one of the necessary characteristics of the Christian church. It is not God's plan that the Christian live in isolation. When the building is used as a tool, it not only is used for worship and evangelism, but it is also a place for Christian instruction and fellowship. Each of these areas is a part of the redemptive ministries in the church.[3]

Although the New Testament gives us no specific direction relative to the design of church buildings or even any information regarding their importance, our use of the buildings as tools makes it possible for us to reveal our theological beliefs and express our faith.

Gathering for Fellowship

Before we ever enter the sanctuary, there should be provisions made to insure that our worship experience will be satisfactory. A wise approach to building can assist us here.

We need to recognize that the average worshiper who comes to our church on Sunday is not necessarily emotionally prepared to immediately enter into a meaningful worship encounter. He may have had a disagreement with a family member before driving to church, found that he was running too late for the second cup of coffee, and encountered a red light at every intersection. Since he is all keyed up, hopefully when he enters the parking lot at the church, he will be able to go immediately to a parking space without further aggravation.

In his seminars on church growth, Robert Schuller strongly emphasizes the need for surplus parking. This represents a technique which demonstrates our desire that any barrier to a person's coming for fellowship be removed.

Upon our worshiper's entry into the building, it is desirable that he discover an attractive area where he can greet fellow worshipers in a sort of neutral spot before going to the location of worship or instruction. During this period in the foyer a sense of community may develop, thus better preparing him for the spiritual experience yet awaiting in the sanctuary.

I doubt that we can emphasize too strongly the need for a large amount of space in the foyer. Not only does this space allow for mingling with people when coming to church, but it also makes possible an extension of the joyful fellowship experienced in the sanctuary when the service is concluded.

Adequate space allows worshipers to remain and enter into conversation with Christian friends.

Not long ago I visited a church where this aspect of church architecture had been overlooked. As the people exited the sanctuary, they were crowded into such a small area that if anyone paused, a mammoth traffic jam would result. Such a situation does not contribute to the atmosphere necessary for fellowship growth.

Special provision should also be made for handicapped and elderly people. The design can be made barrier-free, thus assuring that they are not prevented in any way from full participation in the fellowship gathering.

The Sanctuary, an Aid to Community and Worship

More and more churches are designing their sanctuaries so that the seating is either semicircular or fan-shaped. This design has some very special advantages in that it produces a greater feeling of togetherness. Also even those in the rear seats are much closer to the front than in the traditional long rectangular design.

In our churches where the open-altar concept is employed, a continental plan of seating can be very helpful. With this plan, "individual seats with self-rising bottoms, at 44 to 46-inch spacing back to back, allow best movement in and out of a row. Each seating row thus becomes an aisle."[4] Not only does this arrangement provide for comfort, but it eliminates the need to leave a seat in the middle of a row and have to climb over several people to go forward for prayer.

Special attention needs to be given to provision of good sound quality. It should be possible for the worshiper to hear what is going on at a comfortable volume level. Good design plus adequate sound equipment will be important to accomplish this objective.

Also the design should take into account that congregational singing is important to the feeling of community. Too many sound-absorbing materials in the sanctuary will destroy this effect. Other aspects of design such as shape of room or extreme height of ceiling may contribute to a deadness of sound which is detrimental to the goal of vibrant congregational involvement in the singing.

Particular care should be exercised not to design a sanctuary situation which dwarfs the crowd. Schaller speaks to this concern:

> The members come together every Sunday morning to celebrate the resurrection of Jesus Christ and experience a psychological defeat as two-thirds of the seats are empty. In simple terms, one very effective means of keeping your church from growing is to place your trust in architectural evangelism rather than in person-to-person evangelism.[5]

There is a group of persons who attend our churches and receive minimal benefit because they are unable to hear what is going on. New developments in the field of sound have opened up new avenues of help for these hard-of-hearing. Individual receivers may be used anywhere in the sanctuary, and thus they are not forced to sit in a special location with other hearing-impaired persons. Making this kind of equipment available is a part of our caring-sharing ministry.

The interior design of the sanctuary is of great importance as it may enable us to feel comfortable in God's presence and with His people. We should, in cooperation with the architect, seek to build in such a way as to help our people experience a sense of community.

Utilizing What We Have

For a great many the opportunity of building a new building to accommodate our objectives may not be forthcoming. In this regard, Allen and Parker have said, "Maybe you do not have the building you would like, but be sure the one you have is as clean and as attractive as you can make it."[6]

There are a great many improvements which could be profitably made to many existing structures which would greatly enhance the effectiveness of that church in reaching people. Sometimes we have become so accustomed to the building in which we worship that we fail to see those areas of improvement which need to be made.

Not long ago I entered a sanctuary that I had always considered rather drab and uninviting. To my pleasant surprise a good architect had been consulted and at a fairly reasonable cost, the sanctuary had been given a face-lift. The result was that an old sanctuary interior now had the appearance of a new interior. I suspect that the people who worship there on Sundays have been assisted in their worship experience by this fine provision.

Whether we find ourselves in the enviable position of fashioning a new plant which accommodates all the envisioned demands or we are forced to be content with limited alterations to an existing structure, we must be ever sensitive to the need to utilize what we have to the fullest extent as we pursue the building of a caring-sharing community of believers.

Epilogue

Seated in a circle were the nine members of our newly formed church growth task force. Represented within the group's composition were most of the church's age-groups. The period of time these persons had been associated with the congregation varied widely from charter member status to a young adult with less than two year's tenure.

Across more than 30 years, fairly consistent growth had occurred but now the church had plateaued in its growth cycle. This group was responding to the challenge to determine the next steps we would be required to take if we were to continue as a vital force in the community.

Discussion soon centered upon those factors which had attracted the group's members to this body of believers and had sustained their interest. Mentioned were a strong commitment to the proclamation of the message of scriptural holiness, an atmosphere which indicated genuine concern for one another, a variety of ministries which related to a wide range of family needs, a unique outreach program which had impacted at a particular changepoint in life, and appreciation for a pastor who had successfully ministerd in a time of crisis. Clearly no one element seemed to surface as the common denominator of initial attraction to the church, but all agreed it was the sense of community (koinonia) that contributed most strongly to their continued satisfaction and fulfillment in the local body.

A recent national poll reveals that a vast number of unchurched Americans would respond to the church and its message if they were invited. Couple this potential responsiveness with the challenge of the Great Commission and our mandate becomes quite clear.

Our neighborhoods are filled with people who are plagued by the fear of nuclear destruction, who struggle with the consequences of family deterioration, who live in constant anxiety related to doubtful job security in a confused economic environment, who face the horrible thoughts of freezing to death due to rapidly spiraling energy costs, and who feel that no one cares. What an opportunity for the church to reach out to these troubled persons for whom Christ died and introduce them to a caring-sharing community of believers! We have something to offer them and in turn they can enrich our lives.

The task has never been simple nor is it today. Yet amidst the complexities of building a dynamic fellowship, there emerges an immense satisfaction when we have ministered to revealed needs and the world looking on observes God's love at work in a caring-sharing community of believers.

Notes

Chapter 1

1. Lee Haines, "Genesis," *Wesleyan Bible Commentary* (Grand Rapids: William B. Eerdmans Publishing Co., 1964), 1:34.

2. W. T. Purkiser, ed., *The Church in a Changing World* (Kansas City: Beacon Hill Press of Kansas City, 1973), p. 14.

3. Ibid., p. 48.

4. George A. Buttrick, ed., *The Interpreter's Bible* (New York: Abingdon Press, 1953), 10:425.

5. Donald L. Bubna, *Building People* (Wheaton, Ill.: Tyndale House Publishers, 1978), p. 92.

6. Gary W. Kuhne, *The Dynamics of Discipleship Training* (Grand Rapids: Zondervan Publishing House, 1978), p. 150.

7. Bubna, p. 80.

8. Richard S. Taylor, "Hebrews," *Beacon Bible Commentary* (Kansas City: Beacon Hill Press of Kansas City, 1967), 10:48.

Chapter 2

1. Paul S. Rees, *Don't Sleep Through the Revolution* (Waco, Tex.: Word Books, 1969), p. 37.

2. Samuel M. Shoemaker, *Revive Thy Church Beginning with Me* (Waco, Tex.: Word Books, 1948), p. 28.

3. Donald A. McGavran and Winfield Arn, *Ten Steps for Church Growth* (San Francisco: Harper and Row, 1977), p. 58.

4. Hollis L. Green, *Why Churches Die* (Minneapolis: Bethany Fellowship, 1972), p. 21.

5. Rees, p. 27.

6. Paul Benjamin, *The Growing Congregation* (Cincinnati: Standard Publishing Co., 1972), p. 28.

7. Kenneth Chafin, *Help! I'm a Layman* (Waco, Tex.: Word Books, 1966), p. 103.

8. Donald A. McGavran and Winfield Arn, *How to Grow a Church* (Glendale, Calif.: Gospel Light Publications, 1974), p. 105.

9. Ibid., pp. 3-33.

10. Benjamin, p. 63.

11. George W. Webber, *God's Colony in Man's World* (New York: Abingdon Press, 1960), p. 57.

Chapter 3

1. Leslie Parrott, *Building Today's Church* (Grand Rapids: Baker Book House, 1973), p. 145.

2. Bubna, p. 73.

3. Donald J. MacNair, *The Growing Local Church* (Grand Rapids: Canon Press, 1975), p. 171.

4. Parrott, pp. 145-46.

Chapter 4

1. Robert C. Girard, *Brethren, Hang Loose* (Grand Rapids: Zondervan Publishing House, 1972), p. 131.

2. McGavran and Arn, *How to Grow a Church,* p. 161.

3. Benjamin, p. 53.

4. Howard A. Snyder, *The Problem of Wine Skins* (Downers Grove, Ill.: InterVarsity Press, 1975), p. 141.

5. Lyle E. Schaller, *Assimilating New Members* (Nashville: Abingdon Press, 1978), p. 77.

6. Kuhne, pp. 146-47.

7. Webber, p. 75.

8. Webber, p. 56.

9. Snyder, p. 144.

10. Orville W. Jenkins, *The Church Winning Sunday Nights* (Kansas City: Nazarene Publishing House, 1961), pp. 33-35.

Chapter 5

1. Chafin, p. 98.

2. Charles L. Chaney and Ron S. Lewis, *Design for Church Growth* (Nashville: Broadman Press, 1977), pp. 175-76.

3. Lyle E. Shaller and Charles A. Tidwell, *Creative Church Administration* (Nashville: Abingdon Press, 1975), p. 121.

4. Ibid., p. 123.

5. Chafin, p. 97.

6. Michael Green, *Called to Serve* (Philadelphia: Westminster Press, 1964), p. 18.

7. James L. Garlow, *Partners in Ministry* (Kansas City: Beacon Hill Press of Kansas City, 1981), p. 48.

8. John B. Nielson, *Ministering to Adults Today* (Kansas City: Beacon Hill Press of Kansas City, 1979), p. 71.

9. Charlie W. Shedd, *How to Develop a Praying Church* (New York: Abingdon Press, 1964), p. 43.

10. Bubna, p. 78.

Chapter 6

1. James Earl Massey, *The Worshiping Church* (Anderson, Ind.: Warner Press, 1961), pp. 34-35.

2. MacNair, *The Growing Local Church*, p. 166.

3. Ray C. Stedman, *Body Life* (Glendale, Calif.: Gospel Light Publications, 1972), p. 86.

4. Gene A. Getz, *Sharpening the Focus of the Church* (Chicago: Moody Press, 1974), p. 77.

5. Hollis L. Green, p. 95.

Chapter 7

1. Leonard Griffith, *We Have This Ministry* (Waco, Tex.: Word Books, 1973), p. 37.

2. Eugene L. Stowe, *The Ministry of Shepherding* (Kansas City: Beacon Hill Press of Kansas City, 1976), p. 107.

3. Larry L. Lewis, *Organize to Evangelize* (Wheaton, Ill.: Scripture Press Publications, 1980), p. 17.

4. Lawrence O. Richards, *A New Face for the Church* (Grand Rapids: Zondervan Publishing House, 1970), p. 225.

5. Getz, p. 123.

6. J. Oswald Sanders, *Spiritual Leadership* (Chicago: Moody Press, 1967), p. 65.

7. Robert H. Schuller, *Your Church Has Real Possibilities* (Glendale, Calif.: Gospel Light Publications, 1974), p. 139.

8. C. Peter Wagner, *Your Church Can Grow* (Glendale, Calif.: Gospel Light Publications, 1976), p. 59.

9. Girard, p. 90.

10. Parrott, p. 39.

Chapter 8

1. Anne Ortlund, *Up with Worship* (Glendale, Calif.: Gospel Light Publications, 1975), p. 28.

2. Girard, p. 85.

3. Parrott, p. 104.

4. Wagner, *Your Church Can Grow*, p. 97.

5. Ortlund, pp. 119-20.

6. Ibid., p. 120.

Chapter 9

1. Garlow, pp. 166-67.

2. Edward R. Dayton and Ted W. Engstrom, *Strategy for Leadership* (Old Tappan, N.J.: Fleming H. Revell Co., 1979), p. 67.

3. Ibid., pp. 134-35.

4. Schaller and Tidwell, p. 107.

5. Parrott, p. 41.

6. Jenkins, pp. 57-58.

Chapter 10

1. Lyle E. Schaller, *Hey, That's Our Church!* (Nashville: Abingdon Press, 1975), p. 114.

2. Lyle E. Schaller, *Survival Tactics in the Parish* (Nashville: Abingdon Press, 1977), p. 90.

3. Ralph Stoody, *A Handbook of Church Public Relations* (New York: Abingdon Press, 1959), p. 187.

4. W. Curry Mavis, *Advancing the Smaller Local Church* (Winona Lake, Ind.: Light and Life Press, 1957), p. 117.

Chapter 11

1. Wagner, *Your Church Can Grow*, pp. 110-11.

2. Stedman, p. 23.

3. Massey, p. 25.

4. C. Peter Wagner, *Our Kind of People* (Atlanta: John Knox Press, 1979), p. 33.

5. Ibid., p. 32.

6. Paul R. Orjala, *Get Ready to Grow* (Kansas City: Beacon Hill Press of Kansas City, 1978), p. 49.

7. Ibid., p. 50.

8. McGavran and Arn, *How to Grow a Church*, p. 52.

9. Hollis L. Green, p. 167.

10. Richards, p. 54.

Chapter 12

1. Benjamin, p. 54.

2. Snyder, p. 67.

3. C. Ray Bowman, ed., *Church Building Sourcebook 2* (Kansas City: Beacon Hill Press of Kansas City, 1982), Sec. 1, p. 2.

4. Ibid., pp. 59-60.

5. Schaller, *Assimilating New Members*, pp. 58-59.

6. Charles L. Allen and Mildred Parker, *How to Increase Your Sunday School Attendance* (Old Tappan, N.J.: Fleming H. Revell Co., 1979), p. 69.

Bibliography

Allen, Charles L. and Mildred Parker. *How to Increase Your Sunday School Attendance.* Old Tappan, N.J.: Fleming H. Revell Co., 1979.

Belew, M. Wendell. *Churches and How They Grow.* Nashville: Broadman Press, 1971.

Benjamin, Paul. *The Growing Congregation.* Cincinnati: Standard Publishing, 1972.

Bowman, C. Ray, ed. *Church Building Sourcebook 2.* Kansas City: Beacon Hill Press of Kansas City, 1982.

Bubna, Donald L. *Building People Through a Caring, Sharing Fellowship.* Wheaton: Tyndale House Publishers, 1978.

Buttrick, George A., ed. *The Interpreter's Bible.* New York: Abingdon Press, 1953.

Chafin, Kenneth. *Help! I'm a Layman.* Waco, Tex.: Word Books, 1966.

Chaney, Charles L. and Ron S. Lewis. *Design for Church Growth.* Nashville: Broadman Press, 1977.

Chitwood, Billy J. *What the Church Needs Now.* Old Tappan, N.J.: Fleming H. Revell Co., 1973.

Dayton, Edward R. and Ted W. Engstrom. *Strategy for Leadership.* Old Tappan, N.J.: Fleming H. Revell Co., 1979.

Dolloff, Eugene Dinsmore. *A Crowded Church.* New York: Fleming H. Revell Co., 1946.

DuBose, Francis M. *How Churches Grow in an Urban World.* Nashville: Broadman Press, 1978.

Ellison, H. L. *The Household Church.* Fort Washington, Pa.: Paternoster Press, 1963.

Falwell, Jerry, and Elmer Towns. *Church Aflame.* Nashville: Impact Books, 1971.

Fisher, Wallace E. *Preface to Parish Renewal.* Nashville and New York: Abingdon Press, 1968.

Gangel, Kenneth O. *Competent to Lead.* Chicago: Moody Press, 1974.

Garlow, James L. *Partners in Ministry.* Kansas City: Beacon Hill
Press of Kansas City, 1981.

Getz, Gene A. *Sharpening the Focus of the Church.* Chicago: Moody
Press, 1974.

Girard, Robert C. *Brethren, Hang Loose.* Grand Rapids: Zondervan
Publishing House, 1972.

Green, Hollis L. *Why Churches Die.* Minneapolis: Bethany Fellowship, 1972.

Green, Michael. *Called to Serve.* Philadelphia: Westminster Press,
1964.

Griffith, Leonard. *We Have This Ministry.* Waco, Tex.: Word Books,
1973.

Gundry, Stanley N. *Love Them In.* Chicago: Moody Press, 1976.

Haines, Lee. "Genesis," *Wesleyan Bible Commentary.* Grand Rapids:
William B. Eerdmans Publishing Co., 1964.

Hendricks, Howard G. *Say It with Love.* Wheaton: Scripture Press
Publications, 1972.

Jenkins, Orville W. *The Church Winning Sunday Nights.* Kansas City:
Nazarene Publishing House, 1961.

Kelly, Dean M. *Why Conservative Churches Are Growing.* New York:
Harper and Row, Publishers, 1972.

Kuhne, Gary W. *The Dynamics of Discipleship Training.* Grand Rapids: Zondervan Publishing House, 1978.

Lewis, Larry L. *Organize to Evangelize.* Wheaton: Scripture Press
Publications, 1980.

Lewis, V. H. *The Church Winning Souls.* Kansas City: Nazarene Publishing House, 1960.

Lindsey, Homer G. *How We're Building a New Testament Church.*
Orlando, Fla.: Daniels Publishers, 1975.

MacNair, Donald J. *The Birth, Care, and Feeding of the Local Church.*
Grand Rapids: Canon Press, 1971.

————. *The Growing Local Church.* Grand Rapids: Canon Press,
1975.

Massee, J. C. *Evangelism in the Local Church.* Philadelphia: Judson
Press, 1939.

Massey, James Earl. *The Worshiping Church.* Anderson, Ind.: Warner
Press, 1961.

Mavis, W. Curry. *Advancing the Smaller Local Church.* Winona Lake,
Ind.: Light and Life Press, 1957.

McGavran, Donald A. and Winfield Arn. *How to Grow a Church.* Glendale: Gospel Light Publications, 1974.

———. *Ten Steps for Church Growth.* San Francisco: Harper and Row, 1977.

Nielson, John B. *Ministering to Adults Today.* Kansas City: Beacon Hill Press of Kansas City, 1979.

Orjala, Paul R. *Get Ready to Grow.* Kansas City: Beacon Hill Press of Kansas City, 1978.

Ortlund, Anne. *Up with Worship.* Glendale, Calif.: Gospel Light Publications, 1975.

Parrott, Leslie. *Building Today's Church.* Grand Rapids: Baker Book House, 1973.

Purkiser, W. T., ed. *The Church in a Changing World.* Kansas City: Beacon Hill Press of Kansas City, 1973.

Rees, Paul S. *Don't Sleep Through the Revolution.* Waco, Tex.: Word Books, 1969.

Richards, Lawrence O. *A New Face for the Church.* Grand Rapids: Zondervan Publishing House, 1970.

Sanders, J. Oswald. *Spiritual Leadership.* Chicago: Moody Press, 1967.

Schaller, Lyle E. *Assimilating New Members.* Nashville: Abingdon Press, 1978.

———. *Hey, That's Our Church!* Nashville: Abingdon Press, 1975.

———. *The Pastor and the People.* Nashville: Abingdon Press, 1973.

———. *Survival Tactics in the Parish.* Nashville: Abingdon Press, 1977.

———. *Understanding Tomorrow.* Nashville: Abingdon Press, 1976.

Schaller, Lyle E. and Charles A. Tidwell. *Creative Church Administration.* Nashville: Abingdon Press, 1974.

Schuller, Robert H. *Your Church Has Real Possibilities.* Glendale, Calif.: Gospel Light Publications, 1974.

Shedd, Charlie W. *How to Develop a Praying Church.* New York: Abingdon Press, 1964.

Shoemaker, Samuel M. *Revive Thy Church Beginning with Me.* Waco, Tex.: Word Books, 1948.

Snyder, Howard A. *The Problem of Wine Skins.* Downers Grove, Ill.: InterVarsity Press, 1975.

Stedman, Ray C. *Body Life.* Glendale, Calif.: Gospel Light Publications, 1972.

Stoody, Ralph. *A Handbook of Church Public Relations.* New York: Abingdon Press, 1959.

Stowe, Eugene L. *The Ministry of Shepherding.* Kansas City: Beacon Hill Press of Kansas City, 1976.

Taylor, Richard S. "Hebrews," *Beacon Bible Commentary.* Kansas City: Beacon Hill Press of Kansas City, 1967.

Terry, Lindsay. *Making Church News Known.* Orlando, Fla.: Daniels Publishing Co., 1968.

Wagner, C. Peter. *Our Kind of People.* Atlanta: John Knox Press, 1979.

————. *Your Church Can Grow.* Glendale, Calif.: Gospel Light Publications, 1976.

Webber, George W. *God's Colony in Man's World.* New York: Abingdon Press, 1960.

Womack, David A. *Breaking the Stained Glass Barrier.* New York: Harper and Row, 1973.

————. *The Pyramid Principle.* Minneapolis: Bethany Fellowship, 1977.